WHEN THAT DAY COMES
Training for the Fight

CHRISTOPHER HOYER
with **NATALIE JUNE REILLY**

For David, Kristin, and the babies.

In memory of Police Officer David Van Glasser #8144,

a pillar of strength in life and in death.

"I love you!"

PRAISE FOR *WHEN THAT DAY COMES*
By Christopher Hoyer with Natalie June Reilly

"Hoyer gives a blow-by-blow, day-by-day account of his years in law enforcement. From a drifting teen to his life as a street cop, to present day Marine Corps Police Academy instructor, he has been a constant and ever-ready protector standing between the unlawful and those in need. Part biography, part "how to," this ride-along, real-life story will not let you go. Something special here! On the edge of your seat drama ... this personal story will stay with you long after the book is closed."

—Susan, The Bay Books Coronado

ACKNOWLEDGMENTS

As a survivor of a very unexpected and rewarding career, I wrote this book for a few specific and special reasons. Firstly, I want to honor the memory of all fallen Law Enforcement Officers, but one in particular. Secondly, I hope to pass on what 20 years on the street has taught me and share with you what I believe it takes to survive a career mentally, physically, and emotionally in the field of law enforcement and beyond. I would be remiss not to include *all* of those who put their lives on the line for our country and our community, those everyday sheepdogs, including our fine military and fire rescue personnel who never run from the bullies or the bullets, but rather run toward the fire and the fray to protect the flock.

This book is written for David's Mom, Dad, and very generous squad mates, as well as the good people of the community he laid down his life for. It is also written for those who help the front-line warriors survive day-to-day with their voices, their ears, and their arms. You know who you are.

Thank you!

It would be impossible for me to thank everyone who has helped me throughout my life and my career, but again … you know who you are, and I thank you!

The event that changed my life, and the lives of so many others, is maybe the epicenter of this book. When "that day" came for me, it brought with it a gunfight of epic proportion with every conceivable scenario, emotion, and life-altering outcome. It was so much worse than I could have ever imagined.

Having said that, I chose the title of this book carefully, on the premise that training for the unknown in any career is important and potentially life-changing. When "that day" came, *my* day, all the training and preparation was still not enough. *That* day was where my education truly began. Within these pages, you will read tales of my life as an Officer—on and off the street. Some are long. Some are short. Some will leave you welled up with tears and others laughter. **It is real life.** Nothing in these pages is made up or fictionalized. This is the story of an average street Cop doing a job that on some days seemed damn near impossible.

PROLOGUE
The Day it Happened

Twenty years and 64 days. That was long enough for me. Among my peers, I was labeled the resident "shit magnet" in three separate precincts. I was not reaching for that goal, but over time it became a badge of honor, of sorts, one that I took pride in. I would hold many badges throughout my career in law enforcement. As a Street Cop, I was honored to do so!

This is me, Christopher Matthew Hoyer, otherwise known as "Shit Magnet." This term is used in enforcement and dispatch settings. It generally means things are rolling along smoothly until a certain Cop arrives on scene. Bad shit happens when this asshole is on duty. Most shit magnets are not only aware of their precondition to attract problems for their department or shift but are quite proud of it.

I got a lot of attention on the street. Some folks were entertained, if not amused by my incredible luck. Others were waiting for me to screw up. I may have pandered to both audiences, but overall, I made a habit out of doing the job right. At the end of the day, I was great at catching, but not so much at cleaning. Processing and report-writing was not really my specialty. Dispatch would call me out by my first name over the radio, which was strictly out of policy.

"Christopher!"

I heard that a few times in my career. It was code for: *You should probably mellow out!* Sometimes, just for fun, I would switch channels and announce my intentions when crossing precinct boundaries. Often, Dispatch would scold, "Do **not** start anything over here, Mister!"

Yes, Ma'am!

I have only had one Dispatcher quit because of my antics. It wasn't **really** my fault-ish. It was typical patrol stuff and misinterpreting "illegals" being dropped off for a drug deal, in which case led to three separate foot pursuits, two of which ended in physical fights. Two cars fled the scene, so I requested a helicopter and a K9 unit. I guess it was all too much for the Dispatcher to handle. As soon as we were secure, I was told she dropped her headset and quit right there on the spot.

Sorry! That was not my intention.

Radio codes differ from place to place. Most agencies around the country use the ten-codes with some variation, but beyond that I think they are, more or less, agency specific, albeit somewhat similar between cities for cross-patching purposes. One of my favorite codes was the "suspicious person." After a short time on the street, having developed strong "on-view" skills in respect to spotting and chasing bad guys, I found that, for me, they were *all* suspicious.

These suspicious person calls were like a game of Mad Libs®. They all pretty much sounded the same except for the varying verbs and adverbs attached to them. On average, the suspicious person call occurred at least once a shift. Because of my suspicious nature, a good buddy/squad mate of mine coined a word just for me. I remember it clearly. We were cruising the streets one day when I identified my target. I turned to my squad mate and said, "Hey, man! You see that guy?"

I'll never forget his response.

"Dude, they can't *all* be Chris-picious!"

Chris-picious?

WTF?

We had a good laugh over that one, but the nickname stuck. Over the years I accumulated many nicknames within the department, as well as on the street, including: Snaggle-toothed Bastard, the Hoyer-nator,

Aluminum Man (The PD's answer to Iron Man), and Skinny-Little-Pot-Bellied-Faggot. That one was my personal favorite. Thank you to all my friends and co-workers for the love, but if it's all the same, I think I will stick with Shit Magnet.

The best way for me to begin my story is at the end, at the most significant, memorable, life-altering and, ultimately, career-ending moment. Bear with me, as I struggle to put these words down on the page. The emotional toll has been a challenge.

May 18, 2016: It was a Wednesday—plain clothes week. Not one thing about that day was different than any other—yet. Early in the day I contacted a kid, kind of stupid as it turned out. He could not understand why having a driver's license and car insurance was important, so instead of simply thanking me for submitting charges versus booking him that day, he questioned me.

"It's only a dime bag, dude," he scoffed. "What's the big deal?"

Dude?

"It's a felony, Jackass! Would you rather go to jail?"

I cut the kid loose. Call it laziness, loss of interest or perhaps even a premonition. Who knows what the reason was?

Fast forward to 1430 hours—I was sitting at the station, impounding the kid's weed, planning to ride out the rest of the day and then the call comes out—emergency traffic. It's a burglary. Responding units switch to channel. Not paying attention at all, since the location was out of my area and about 15 miles away, my lieutenant got on the air asking for a plain clothes unit to head to the area and scout the house. Shit! It was only 2:30 in the afternoon. I still had time to get into something.

Dumbass!

I hopped in the undercover hot rod and sped away, asking for pertinent information that I missed having switched over late. There were very, very few details. Basically, a guy with a death wish showed up and kicked in the door to his father's home and stole his gun.

Okay ... nothing special.

Wait! He is suicidal and plans a shootout with the Cops? That upped the ante, but it was still not blowing up my skirt. I got instructions from the sergeant to head over to the house while they spoke with the father down the street.

"Yes sir!"

Here is the information I had:

➢ A van in the driveway

➢ No movement

➢ No foot traffic or vehicle traffic of any kind

➢ Average working-class neighborhood

> Cookie-cutter houses

> Nothing out of the ordinary, even for the trained eye

Not much to report.

Looking back, however, it was ***too*** quiet, eerily so.

What I knew:

> The subject was suicidal

> The subject was armed with his dad's handgun

> The subject's last known location was in the house

> Responding units were staging and waiting on my intel

What I did ***not*** know:

> The subject was on two types of amphetamines and THC

> The subject was hiding in the driver's seat of the van

> The subject was prepared to kill and die without hesitation

Usually when we respond to "suicidal" calls, it is met with a yawn and the obligatory, *"Okay. Yeah. We know. You are never going back to jail. Whatever!"*

Personally, I always feared the quiet ones, the ones who just acted, never threatening or whining. The ones that bitched and complained and threatened would usually cower at the sight of a formidable enemy. That being said ... we had a plan in place, a good, solid plan, one that I have picked apart more times than I can count since that day. The plan of attack was based on what we knew at the time. In other words, we acted on the intel we had. Yes, please! Let's dissect other possible ways to remove this bad guy in a box. With hours of strategic-planning, it is possible, however, unlikely, in this case, to come up with a more sound, tactical approach. Remember, our bad guy was armed, suicidal and he wanted a shoot-out with the Cops. What could we have done differently? Well, we could have (and we did have):

> SWAT team on standby

> K9 on the way

> Chopper on the way

> 270-degree coverage around the front of the house

> Undercover unit watching—me

> Uniformed Officers staging to the rear

> Field Training Officers and specialty unit guys on scene

> Cover cars, rifles, and a plan to surround and call out

> A sound plan for patrol-level ability without the toys the TAC guys have

Again, we acted based on what we knew at the time. As law enforcement, it has been drilled into us that "time is on our side." It's sometimes true, but not always. In this case, definitely *not*! And even though we called SWAT, the reality was, we could not call the "big guns" for every suicidal subject. A good friend of mine said it best:

"We're Cops! Sometimes we have to expose ourselves."

So, there I was … on scene—exposed. Thirteen minutes alone, 13 minutes I wish I could do over. I'd like to peer in from the outside, ask the critical questions.

> ➢ Did I miss anything?
>
> ➢ Could I have done more?
>
> ➢ Was there more to see?

These are answers I may never get, at least not until God says so, but do I even want the answers?

Survivor's guilt sucks.

It was bad for everyone on this scene. For me, it was even worse because I watched that house and that van for 13 minutes—13 WHOLE minutes! Not one single thing moved the entire time.

Damn it!

I have tried to forgive myself for failing. That's a lot easier said than done. When I saw the marked units, I disembarked from my undercover car. I was about 30 yards southwest of the house.

I was geared up—ballistic vest, outer carrier fully loaded down:

> ➢ Glock 21 .45 caliber pistol
>
> ➢ Four spare mags

- ➤ Two extra AR15 mags, all within reach

- ➤ Rifle

- ➤ Colt AR15 6920, loaded with 28 rounds

- ➤ Glock 30 in the small of my back

- ➤ Kevlar helmet, earpiece, and gloves

Physically: I was battle-ready.

Ready to rock and roll!

Mentally: I thought I was, but certain things screw you up in these situations. Up to that point in my career, I had been involved in shooting situations. There were three in total: Two bad guys and one dog. The two bad guys were categorized as "shootings." Hence, when the targets turned, I raised and fired two or more rounds, bad guy fell, and I waited for internal affairs and the pizzas. *That's* a shooting! It is a vast difference from a gunfight.

You think?

Again, as a street Cop, I'd been hard-wired for a "shooting." Having previously eliminated the threat (times three), defeating my enemies, I was ready for this battle, not once considering what would happen if it did *not* work in my favor.

Marked cars were heading my way. One car blocked the street to the north. Two more passed, as I moved into position in the street. Two more cars stopped short of the house and, as fate would have it, Officer David Glasser was at the head of the conga line. It was his Tahoe that blocked the van in the driveway. It was a sound tactic. The question for me, weeks and even months later, was what would have happened if we *hadn't* blocked in the van in question? The suspect drives off. A rolling gun battle ensues, ergo a pursuit with a known, armed felon.

The possibilities are endless.

It was a good tactic. Unplanned, perhaps, but as far as I am concerned, it was necessary to block further escape. Parked behind the van, David exited his Tahoe. We didn't know it at the time, but shithead (i.e., our suspect) was in the driver's seat of the van, lying in wait. He must have had a plan, of sorts. He made visual contact with the first Officer he saw— David. Three rounds were fired. David was hit twice. David went down. Gunfire erupted. All hell broke loose, and life, as I knew it, would never be the same.

CHAPTER ONE
Early Lesson in Carrying On

I am the son of a United States Marine, a man I have never met. From what I am told, he was Special Forces—recon. This could explain a lot about who I am, and the career path I pursued. My biological father was deployed to Vietnam in 1969, the year I was born. He was never seen or heard from again, not from the little family he left behind anyway—heartbreaking. That's not to say that I haven't tried to find him. There is a part of me that wonders how different my life would be if he had been around. I guess I'll never know.

My mom is great! I love her. She's a rock star! She provided everything I needed, but it wasn't what I would call a "happy" upbringing. I am not going to say I am disappointed, but it wasn't what I wanted growing up. The truth is, I am no stranger to challenge and the harshness of *real* life. Growing up, I had plenty of both. Life got especially tough in high school. I never got too comfortable at any one school. I transferred in and out of at least four.

1

At 14 years old, a high school freshman, I loved riding my bike. It was the best part of being a kid. The worst part about it was being so impressionable. I had a friend who was less than responsible. He got me into a fair amount of trouble. Being young and unknowing cost me. In many ways, it was the last time in my life when I would enjoy being "free." I remember hopping into a car one night with my friend's adult sister and her boyfriend for an excursion to the mall. We didn't do anything more than drive around, but when I didn't return home, mostly out of fear, Mom was pretty upset. She did not believe me when I told her we were just cruising around all night. I never did convince her of that fact.

"Why did you do this? That was so dangerous and unlike you," she exclaimed. "You're going to live with your father!"

Of course, I cannot ever forget why my Mom is such a bad-ass. I have towered over her since I was 12 years old, but all things considered, I made the near-fatal mistake of responding to her in the heat of the moment.

"Well, at least it was only the first time!"

I'm not sure the handprint ever really went away. I got slapped so hard I think it scared my unborn kids.

Sorry, Mom.

Not long after that, I went to live with my stepdad. He is the only father figure I ever knew. His was a short-lived marriage to Mom, ending

2

abruptly. He was a stand-up man, supporting Mom and me when times called for it. Again, not ideal, but those were the cards I was dealt, and I am grateful for him, nonetheless.

When I turned 15, I was employable. I worked full-time throughout the summer, including weekends. That was a shock to the system, to say the least. When school started up again, it was a new and unwanted chapter in my life. Besides the fact that this was high school number three for me, it was an hour long commute every day to a school aptly nicknamed the "Cow Barn."

*What do you think **that** means?*

On top of which, at the end of the school day, I had to wait on campus until I got picked up or I found a place to go, whichever came first. Lucky for me, I found a friend and was able to hang out at his house. Of course, then there was the hour-long drive home. It was taxing on everybody. As a kid, I remember thinking that summertime meant I was finally free from school, teachers, and homework. That feeling of freedom came to a grinding halt when I was told I would be up at seven o'clock every morning throughout the summer and would be given a long list of chores to complete.

That will take me all day! And you want me to do this every day?

WTF?

Goodbye, summer!

After a year of that nonsense, I was asked, "Would you like to go back to a 'normal' public school?"

You mean, like in a real city? Ummmmm ... YEAH!

That's when I enrolled in high school number four. It was goodbye to the "Cow Barn" and back to a regular school, as regular as possible in the New England area. It was one of those "it sounded great in the brochure" situations in the middle of nowhere, in some godforsaken forest—deep, deep in the forest. The house we lived in was set in an amazing location for a summer camp or a vacation rental right on the lake, but for full-time living it was tough, especially for a city kid who knew nothing of responsibility. I was contending with mosquitoes that rivaled pterodactyls in the summer and, in the winter, the snow was so deep you had to carry a flare gun and an emergency survival kit to the end of the driveway—not that you could drive. The plows would block in the driveway with mountains of snow every stinking morning, as they scraped it out of the roadway. And you would need at least a 30-minute head-start to warm up the car. And who do you think got tasked with this? Me.

Best of all was the mile-long walk to the bus stop. And no one believes me, but it was uphill BOTH ways AND in the snow! AND in the dark! AND barefoot!

Okay. I made that part up, but gimme a break!

Add the one hour and 15-minute bus ride to school and I was the first kid on in the morning and the last one off in the afternoon.

Jeez!

For the most part, things were mellow until the beginning of my senior year. A few weeks into the semester, everything changed for the worse. I was 18 years old. I had a total POS car, but it was mine. Unlike my junior year when I was Mr. Popularity, a stellar athlete who was dating the head cheerleader, my senior year was rough. It was a game of catch up. I had to complete a full class load in order to graduate. Being **responsible** was the priority at home, so I was working full-time, too. I thought I had a decent handle on things. Not so much, as it turned out. That's when I was told, "If you want to live here, you have to pay rent."

Come again?

This was the moment that changed my life forever. It was a Saturday morning. I was sitting at the dining room table eating a bowl of cereal. Dad walked in, sat down, and opened the newspaper. I thought nothing of it.

"You have your rent money," he asked.

"Nope."

"Where you gonna live?"

"I don't know," I shrugged.

That's when reality hit. I was on my own, so I stood up, and placed the cereal bowl in the sink. I packed a couple bags of clothes, making two trips to the car. On the second trip, there was a bag of groceries waiting for me. I picked up the groceries, got into my POS car and drove off—no fight, no tears, and no goodbye. That's how quickly life as I knew it came to an end. The entire event took about 15 minutes. I did not defy my parents. They said it and I did it. There was no ceremony. I just left. It was just that simple. What else could I do?

Over the years, there have been some lasting struggles with getting booted from both of my homes at such a young age, but I dealt with the demons and faced the reality of how harsh life could be. The fact was the level of responsibility put on me at the time was simply too much. I don't blame anyone for this because life is not easy, and the lesson learned was a good one. As a naïve kid, I was just not ready for it. Needless to say, graduating high school was not going to happen and the idea of being instantly homeless was a new concept. Where does one go from there? Podunk New England in the deep woods in the mid 80s wasn't exactly a hot bed for hotels. So, again, the questions lingered: Where? Who? What? How? It was just me. This was my first realization that I would truly have to fend for myself, carry my own weight.

After weeks of living in my car, I found a buddy who let me stay with him for a spell, which was fortunate because my POS car died and was instantly towed.

Thanks a lot!

I never saw it again. I was, however, able to see my dad again. I maintained contact with him, and I went back "home" to visit Mom that Thanksgiving. Home? The truth was I had lost sight of what *home* was for me. I looked at this opportunity of starting over with the shame of becoming a high school dropout. I didn't let that emotion hang around for long. I kept moving forward, even though it was a tough struggle, bouncing from place to place to place. I did, however, find a little solace in a new job. I worked hard and before long I was back on my feet. I saved up enough money for an apartment and soon after a new hot rod. Life got easier. I was fending for myself on a whole new level and the decisions I was making were now based on success, not survival.

FROM CARPET LAYER TO COP

#6807

At 26 years old, I was married and running a small construction company out west—flooring repair. The work was not what I would consider rewarding, but being a small business owner was pretty cool. It paid the bills. I had a four-year-old daughter, an angel of a girl with a future for greatness in mind. Life was progressing as it should.

One boring day in 1996, I got a call from a prospective client.

"Can you fix the mess in my entry way," he asked.

"Sure! I'll be right over," I responded eagerly.

After two weeks of negotiating, we reached a deal and he finally agreed to hire me. When we met face-to-face, he seemed a little surprised.

"Where's your boss? Shouldn't I be speaking with him?"

In other words, how old are you?

"Well, sir, that's me!" I replied. "I assume my crew leader introduced himself properly."

"You're the boss?" he smiled, shaking my hand.

"Yes, sir!"

Two days (and two weeks) later, the work was complete. The man paid me for a job well done and then he made a comment that changed the trajectory of my life, both personally and professionally.

"You're a terrific individual! You should be a Cop."

Eh? Me? Okay.

As simple as it was, the comment made me think and, honestly, it was not a hard decision to make, considering I was getting pretty sick of rolling around in carpet soaked in disgusting unmentionables. It was back-breaking work that I could not picture myself doing when I was 40 years old. Not to mention, the damage it was doing to my knees and, even worse, my back. For the first time in my life, I began setting goals for myself. And I believe it made all the difference in the long run.

Speaking of long "run!"

On this new path to pursue a career in law enforcement, the endless hours of study began and so did the running. It was all in preparation for the upcoming written and physical exam. I was fully confident that I had it in the bag, until I walked into a massive room at the Civic Center filled with 1,200 other Officer Candidates. Then it hit me.

Yeah right! I have no chance here.

I almost walked out, all 6'1 and 140 pounds of me.

I really wanna do this, right?

"Find a seat! Sit down! Shut up and listen closely," a gruff voice boomed like a cannon from the front of the room. From there, we Officer candidates sat quietly, listening intently to a motivational speech about how great a career in law enforcement could be. The words ricocheted off the walls and into our ears and hearts.

It was very uplifting!

Obviously, the force behind it was by design, a way to get us fired up and motivated to do some serious soul searching. All the while, I nonchalantly sized up my competition, as I suspect most of the other candidates did. There were lots of military types, surely the first to be selected and why wouldn't they be? What had I done to earn that spot? There were other types present. One guy looked to be about 127 years old. Another looked like he hadn't even graduated high school yet. I don't think the guy in the "Will work for sex" t-shirt is going to score any points with this group. It was funny though. I'll give him that. God only knows what these guys were thinking about me. On the outside I looked more like a tweaker than a Cop. Nevertheless, I was there amongst all the rest of the hopefuls and **that was my first fight in law enforcement**, a contest for a career and for a purpose. I couldn't help but think that maybe, just maybe, I could make this work.

CHAPTER TWO
Cops and Robbers

The first time I was asked the question, "So, why do you want to be a Cop," I was in a formal setting in a room full of potential Police new hires.

Me?

"I think it is gonna be fun to chase bad guys, carry a gun and drive as fast as I want! Cops and robbers in the Wild West … right?"

Oh yeah!

SCREECHING HALT!!!

"Umm … Yeah. Son, we are not looking to hire cowboys here. So, let's try this again."

Let us fast forward to a formal meeting with the brass where we conducted Police Academy intros.

"So, recruit, why do you want to be an Officer?"

"Well, sir, I want to rid the world of bad people, so that my daughter and her friends have a safer place to grow up."

Yeah right.

My first answer was the truth, and the truth was I made a career out of having fun. Not all the time, but like they say, when you are working a dream job, it's not work. That's a true story. I would like to believe that I did my share of making the world a bit safer though. I certainly tried. I do have a list of folks who may or may not be back in society who would, let's just say, like to "thank" me for my efforts. To them I'd say, "If you have been reformed, and you are reading this, I hope these words find you. If not … you probably can't read anyway."

THE POLICE ACADEMY
#6807

After working in the property room for two weeks, it was academy time. Waiting for a class to start is commonplace for recruits. There were three or four of us working together. We did a little bit of studying in between our daily duties, mostly trying to figure out what we were in for. The property room is more like a property city block, an enormous warehouse filled to the brim with every imaginable thing. It is like a yard

12

sale for an entire city—impressive and somewhat entertaining. However, there is not much to learn there, at least not for the level of responsibility about to be put on us. Moving heavy objects and painting was not exactly my idea of police work, but it was a means to an end. And, of course, in the meantime, we recruits tried to stay in shape. This was my first venture in failure.

"Hey rookies we're going running! Are you going to join us?"

By the way, when you hear this from a Training Officer, this is **not** a request.

"No, we'll just wait to hear how it went," I joked. "Of course, we're going!*"*

This was my chance to impress the boys … right?

Wrong! Big mistake! The brass **does not** care, nor do they mind letting you know when you've screwed up. It's a good thing I was smart enough to know that if I didn't go on this run, it would look *really* bad. Again, it was not a request.

Physically-speaking, I had some "issues" caused from a career in floor repair. The long and the short of it: I had bad knees and I didn't know how "bad" until the third or fourth long distance run. The mile-and-a-half was all I ever did. Just get past the testing process … right?

Ummm … no!

Now, I admit when I graduated the academy, I was capable of running marathons. Prior to that? Not so much. We're talking an eight-mile trail run, all mountain terrain. Halfway through, I pretty much blew out my knee. Basically, I was running with no tendons—bone on bone. Did I quit like a normal person? No. I kept going because how would it look if I quit? And, of course, I didn't say anything during the run.

See how smart I am?

The first day of academy, physical training was anything but fun, especially when I told the training staff I was physically out of commission. I was extremely fortunate that the knee injury was minor and could be fixed with stretches and lots of ibuprofen, but speaking out put a target on my back.

Better step up.

The academy was *mostly* fun, lots to learn. There was some stuff we recruits questioned as a group, but elected to keep our mouths shut. I was reminded of my stepdad and the times I questioned him, like "When am I ever going to need algebra?"

"Probably never again, but guess what," Dad quipped. "You need it right now."

How does one argue with that logic?

Jeez!

Even I used that line on my own kids and, of course, I laughed my ass off for recycling parental rhetoric.

Meanwhile, back at the academy, I found myself contending with that same logic, as in "I'm not ever going to be a DUI motor Cop, so why am I doing this?

Because right now!

Okay. Shut up and learn!

Oh, and I'm getting *paid* to learn?"

Really! Just shut up, smile, and learn.

That's kind of a big deal, if you think about it—getting paid to learn. I never considered that as a "benefit" when I chose this career, but it certainly didn't hurt. There are many on-the-job-training opportunities in the world of law enforcement. And what could be better than getting paid to learn how to shoot, as well as learn defensive tactics and tactical driving? All good stuff!

Sign me up!

On the first day of academy, something strange happened. One entire state over from ours was a launching site for rocket testing. On that chilly December morning, we were all standing in the parking lot, shivering from anticipation more than the cold, and suddenly, the most beautiful pink image appeared over the open skyline. Not knowing what it was, we all stared in amazement. It wasn't until later that we learned it was rocket testing. I only had one thought, *Is that rocket test symbolic of my new career?* A little fantasy-oriented, but I have to say, I was already feeling quite accomplished just getting to that point. I had no idea where this ride was going to take me. In my mind, it was a wise choice. This career path full of challenges, both good and bad, appeared to be full of life—REAL life! And it was definitely worth the fight to get there.

CHAPTER THREE
The Strong, Silent ... What?

I learned a lot about myself and about self-discipline in the hiring process. Most of all, I learned patience. I had my fair share of life experience. I thought that would help me and it did, to a point. However, the truth of the matter was, I had *no* idea what I was facing. They told me, "You can come back in six weeks and retake the written exam."

"I failed the written exam?"

"Yes ... you did ... by two questions."

Sum-bitch!

Okay. I really want to do this ... right?

KEEP FIGHTING!

Then, again, they told me, "You can come back in six weeks to retake the physical exam."

Damn it!

Stupid sit ups!

And, so, I retested again ... and again and it was only because of my fierce determination and training that I finally made it! There was nothing stopping me.

Right?

Then they told me, "We need you here on Thursday at 10 a.m."

"Yes sir!"

I was in the parking lot at nine o'clock in the morning—sharp. At ten minutes to 10:00 a.m., I was in the office.

"I'm sorry we had an unexpected cancellation. Another guy got your spot. Can you come back at two o'clock?"

"Yes. I can."

At 1:45 p.m. I was back in the office, ready to go.

2:00 p.m.

2:10 p.m.

2:15 p.m.

2:30 p.m.

"Ma'am?"

"Oh!" the woman behind the counter sighed. "I'm sorry! Can we reschedule for two weeks from Monday? He had to leave."

*Okay! Sure. I **really** want to do this. Right?*

KEEP FIGHTING!

Then there was the background check, requiring all kinds of

information, including every job, residence, traffic ticket, vehicles owned, dog, friend, relative and favorite movie. The packet alone took me two weeks to finish, but I got through it, plus …

- ➢ Fingerprints
- ➢ Oral board
- ➢ Formal interview
- ➢ Check-up: Turn your head and cough
- ➢ Blood work
- ➢ Vision test
- ➢ Dental Checkup
- ➢ KY jelly
- ➢ Psych evaluation
- ➢ Firstborn child
- ➢ Mother's maiden name
- ➢ Brainteasers: *A train leaves Denver at 2:00 p.m. and another train leaves Chicago at 6:00 p.m.*
- ➢ And the all-important, non-admissible polygraph test

Okay!

KEEP FIGHTING!

I must admit, once I got through all that mess, I had a newfound confidence. I was good to go!

Just give me my badge and gun and set me free.

As if.

DAY ONE AT THE ACADEMY

━━━━━━━━━ **#6807** ━━━━━━━━━

"Keep your heads up and your mouths shut! Classroom A. Don't you dare be late and don't even *think* about asking how to find it. Find a seat and remain silent!"

Like church mice, our recruit class waited no less than 30 minutes. I lost track of time, but before long we all got the life scared out of us. He was not a big man. He was fit ... *very* fit and somewhat soft-spoken. I do not know who kicked the door open, but holy Christ I thought they were coming after me! I'm sure my 45 recruit buddies all felt the same, as we scrambled to our feet at the command of our class sergeant and his staff of recruit training Officers. I was thinking to myself, *You know, that door is probably expensive, and you just might give someone a heart attack.*

It did not take me long to realize that these folks were going to harass us for all it was worth. Perhaps, even, for their amusement. It wouldn't hit me until a few years later that this was a process. I could already hear Joe Citizen screaming at me, "I pay your salary! You're supposed to protect and serve *me*! It is your job to get shot at, screamed at

20

and spit on, so **SUCK IT UP!**"

Have you any idea the crap I had to endure just to *wear* this uniform? The more I think about it, the more I think I should have gone back to thank the training staff who gave me such a hard time. They mentally prepared me for the street, and I didn't even realize it.

Sneaky little dudes.

The street was easy or, at least, I *thought* it was. My first major incident was the stuff of great story-telling. The **biggest lessons** learned were **attention to detail**, **courage** and **physical willingness**. Physical preparedness, in and of itself, can be a major issue. However, **I believe the biggest building block of all, when it comes to law enforcement, is mental preparedness.** The fact is this profession is made up of the strong, silent type and what we don't talk about can hurt us.

CHAPTER FOUR
My Un-finest Moment

While in the academy, I was personally making decisions based on survival. However, as a class, things were a lot less stressful. Overall, I thought we had a good time. Most of the time, it was not too tough, and our leader was pretty cool. Many of our training Officers were on light-duty, which meant there was not a lot of running, which was fine by us recruits. I mean, it's not like they don't give us patrol cars on the street ... right?

There were not too many surprises, at least as far as the curriculum was concerned. Report-writing, learning to drive fast, shoot a gun, radio etiquette, first-aid, state statutes, criminal law, courtroom testimony and so on. It wasn't until later that I realized what we were lacking in education, which was *how* to actually chase bad guys, the reason most of us were there. But the lessons were thorough enough, and we were all eager to learn. As for the "chasing bad guys" portion ... keep reading. I pictured myself a baby lion. Thanks to the training Officers, I knew how to clean and prep the prey, but I hadn't yet learned *how* to catch it. That's what I really wanted to learn. But first came some hard lessons.

NEVER SHOOT RELOADS

#6807

Since the statute of stupidity has run out, it's probably okay to reveal my biggest mistake as a recruit. By week 12 or 13, I took it upon myself to practice shooting on my own. Some of the recruits were having trouble qualifying with the handguns. Me? I didn't have trouble qualifying, so much as finding out the hard way that some guns do not shoot reloaded ammunition.

Oops!

After a small purchase/repair from a local gun shop and five separate policy violations later, my training weapon was fixed, a friendship was lost, a few threats were made, and I had the most discipline ever handed out in the academy at that point. Imagine if you will a pin-dropping silence on the parade deck. I was just a kid with buckling knees and a growing fear of having to go back to laying carpet.

"Gimme your gun belt," the training sergeant shouted.

We, the senior class were standing at attention up front. There were three classes standing behind mine. The entire staff of academy head sheds stood before me, looks of disgust on their faces—feigned looks, I presume. Not that I dared to look at them.

This was the closest I ever came to passing out. I was told to sit in the lunchroom and keep my mouth shut. Of course, all the other recruits were buzzing about, asking what I had done. The general consensus was, "Oh my God!"

And I didn't think I could feel any worse.

After a couple of hours of deliberation and strategic "punishment planning" and, surely, a whole lot of belly-laughing behind closed doors after the decision had been made, I found myself sitting in the sergeant's office. It was 30 minutes of the worst ass-chewing in history. I did not realize just how low I could actually sink into a chair before that day. The sweetest words I ever heard, at least in a professional setting, (ahem) were, "We decided we are not going to fire you."

An entire Mardi Gras went off in my head. The relief must have shown on my face because the words that followed weren't as comforting. "Don't get too happy just yet. I suggest you buy a new pair of running shoes and a box of pens."

Two 5,000 word essays later, on topics that included "cracking an egg" and "tying your shoes," I had written my way out of that mess. They couldn't give me something complicated to write about, like nuclear fusion and its benefits to world peace? Next came the physical punishment: 150 push-ups and as many sit-ups and ten trail runs. On top of which came the obligatory, but *very* real threat.

"Boy, do not even consider screwing up again!"

"Sir, yes sir!"

In my head I was thinking, *Sir, can you pass me that oxygen bottle? Oh ... and can I shine your shoes for you while I am here? Paint your office? Donate a kidney?*

Let me just say, with that profound experience under my belt, I was aware of how one *really* stupid mistake could put me at risk for losing everything I had worked so hard for. Of course, there were a total of five mistakes, but who was counting? Oh yeah ... the staff!

Damn it!

Lesson learned. I think it really helped me appreciate, a little more, the importance of upholding this responsibility as a professional representative of my community and, of course, my department.

CHAPTER FIVE
Geared Up and Ready to Go

We were informed as a class to prepare to work a swing shift, otherwise known as **the uniformed ride along**. We were told, "This is your time to learn. Do what you're told and do not try to be a hero out there. Got it?"

Sure ... I got it, but what if I **can** *save the world?*

This was the second of two ride alongs. The first ride-along was done in "recruit" gear. It was your basic white, button-down shirt and tie— the worst-of-the-worst of academy attire. The first ride along was not a test. It was nothing more than observing "life on the street" with an experienced Officer. It was also an opportunity for a little more "soul searching."

> ➤ No gun.
>
> ➤ No authority.
>
> ➤ No nada.

We were commanded to sit in the car and observe. The second

ride along was much, MUCH better-ish. My field training officer (FTO) was a seasoned veteran, a man who would later become my mentor. He was a giant of a man. Beyond just his massive build, he was a legend among the FTO community and I, his protégé, was ready for anything. However, as a "wet-behind-the-ears," not even a badge-holding rookie, I did have a gun and I was terrified!

It was a very cold introduction to my FTO. Mostly, he just gave me a hard look—up and down. It was followed by a doubtful smirk, obviously questioning my ability.

"How much do you weigh," he barked.

"Sir, I am 140 pounds."

"With all your gear on or what," he replied coarsely.

Kiss my ass, Bitch!

"No, sir," I said, biting my tongue. "I am a solid 160 geared up!"

"Hmmm ... of course you are," he chuckled. "Let's go, booter!"

That night we transported some guy for whatever reason. He was not a bad guy, but nevertheless, people ***do not*** go in our cars without being searched. This is a practice in due diligence that I whole-heartedly support. Now, having said that, this dude was wearing nothing more than a Speedo and a tank top and it was up to me to search him, just so that we could give him a ride. I got the feeling my FTO was enjoying it. I could see underneath his poker face, he was secretly dazzled with excitement.

Fucker.

I was no more than five minutes into patting this guy down when my FTO says, "Did you check the groin area?"

It was a search that should have taken no more than 60 seconds. However, I spent five whole minutes purposely *avoiding* that particular area. My FTO knew full-well that I had not searched the groin area. I looked over at him. He had a dead serious look on his face. However, I knew for a fact he was laughing his ass off on the inside, watching me squirm while having to perform my duty, a task that would eventually become commonplace in my professional future.

"Damn it! You know I didn't!"

"Ok then ..."

It was not that big of a deal in "real world" terms, but the dude was "*out there.*" If he had anything else in those shorts, I think it would have been time for ... never mind! I'm not going there ... or there! As it turned out, the guy was not carrying anything. I glared at my FTO for the next three hours.

Yeah. Shut up and learn. Right?

I was still in the academy and my *plan* was to go back and tell my classmates that I got to drive the car on two wheels, repel off a building and deliver a baby.

Yeah, man!

In reality, the highlight of my night was that I got to handle another dude's junk. My first day delivering pizzas was not *that* exciting.

I purposefully chose this career. Right?

In the end, I survived the night. I finally had street experience.

Look at me! Top o' the world, Ma!

And yet … I still had *no* idea what was coming.

That was *my* fight!

GEARING UP FOR THE FIGHT

#6807

During the testing phase, I watched as several monster-sized, scary dudes tested against me. Considering their strength and brawn, I was sure they would all be shoe-ins and a lot of them did make it. There were also recruits who were much smaller than me. As it turned out, **physical preparedness** was not too tough to grasp. Practicality was the key. As for comfort … forget it! There was no comfort in 117-degree weather at 1400 hours, not when you had been on perimeter for two hours.

Yeah right! Keep fighting!

You do your best, and you drink a lot of water, which brings me to the importance of gearing up.

Hmmm ...

What does that look like?

> Knife on support side

Check.

> Laces tucked into boots

Check.

> Non-widow-maker holster that does not require time-lock release

Check. Check.

> Secondary weapon that you regularly train on

Check.

> Anything with Velcro, zippers and cool patches that read "The Infidel" or "This is the tool. I am the weapon"

Check.

> Saint Michael medallion somewhere close by

Check.

Hey, every little bit helps! Check.

The **holster** thing was a big deal. Mine was a holster that nearly ended my career and almost my life. I got talked into the "latest and greatest" rig setup, like new Officers often do. We're told something like,

"Okay. The holster is incredibly simple to operate. Begin with a pirouette and then yodel three times. Slap the side of it and then grab the bottom and push at a 45-degree angle and *voila* it is out, and you are good to go!"

Well, I may be over-exaggerating a little, but once upon a time when my partner and I rolled up on an armed robbery suspect, things went bad very quickly. I was the passenger. The dude (i.e., our subject) was walking on my side of the car … away from us. We stopped a few yards behind him and exited the car. Actually, it all happened a little quicker than I expected because oftentimes I had time to prep the holster prior to contact. However, in this case, there was no time.

We were out of the car. My partner delivered the commands. The bad guy spun around and inside his waistband was an Uzi. He was eyeballing me because I was the closest threat, but by the grace of God, he decided not to play, which was good for me because I could not (I repeat: *I could not*) get the gun out of the holster! Had he engaged me, I would have lost—no question about it. Thank God for a competent partner because he was on it and ready to rock and roll.

Thanks, bro!

Needless to say, that rig got tossed. Another wise investment is a **quality weapon mounted light**. If you don't have one, get one. I know what you're going to say, "*But … I work during the day.*" I hear that

31

all the time. Okay. So, you have never entered a dark warehouse in the daytime? How about a bar? Alright! How about one of my worst fears, lifting the covers to look under a bed? Is there light under there?

I think not.

Handheld flashlight?

Nope.

It takes three hands for that.

"Drop it on the floor," you say?

Good tactic ... sometimes, but when "Murphy" steps in and the light rolls away or ends up missing the *one* corner you needed lit?

No.

Secondary Officer?

First off, will there be enough room for two in a tiny bedroom? What if the bed cannot be flipped? Is it too heavy or is the headboard preventing it from moving? The possibilities are endless. The best part, for me, besides the obvious lighting of a darkened area, was putting the light in some dude's eyes and blinding him, usually just long enough for me to gain the advantage I needed.

The **support side knife** tactic was something I learned in the academy. Weapon retention kept on my primary side.

Terrific!

There are *many* ways to defeat an opponent and just as many variables to losing. So, for me, the non-thinking, simplest way was my support side knife. If a bad dude grabbed my gun, then the knife came out and went into his most immediately exposed body part. This indicates deadly force now. Right?

Right.

You've got to be prepared for those "what ifs." And then there's the less obvious piece of equipment—**shoelaces.** I learned (the hard way) that they can get looped onto the gas and brake pedals. It's a sinking feeling, not just because it can negatively alter your driving, but even worse, it could mean getting stuck in the car. If you needed to jump out in a hurry, it could be a problem. And while we're on the subject of driving, I will say that I am religious about wearing **seat belts**—on and off duty.

There are two different times to consider: When to put it on and when to take it off. In this line of work, a seatbelt can be cumbersome depending on the situation. When making a stop, I learned the best time to disengage the seat belt is seconds before coming to an actual stop. It allows you to exit your car more quickly and lessens the chance of getting trapped, so to speak, by an unexpected intruder. There really is no excuse not to wear it while you are driving. Honestly, who has ever been ambushed at 70 miles per hour? I say wear it.

Speaking of driving, my FTO was relentless when it came to keeping the car stocked. He'd say, "Better be gassed up, Rookie! Is that a spot in my view on the windshield? Crumbs on my seat? Mountain Dew can in the cup holder?"

Well, then move your ass and clean it!

Yeah. I pretty much kept that thought to myself, but the truth was I was *horrible* about stocking my car. I was always running out of envelopes or crime scene tape or cones. I had plenty of ammo and tactical stuff though. The one thing I did **not** ever fail on was fuel. I always assumed I would end up chasing some bad guy across the state and how could I ever live it down if he escaped because I decided **not** to gas up.

Not okay.

Months had passed—blood, sweat and tears—for real. I got through it all:

- Written test
- PT test
- Background investigation
- Pre-academy
- Academy
- Post-academy
- Two FTOs

There is a sense of freedom and accomplishment when one rolls solo for the first time. I remember waiting for the precinct gate to open. I was thinking, *Hey, I made it!* **I am the Police**, *but…now what? Where do I go? I know! I'll go show off my new car to my friends.*

Wait! No.

My old boss!

Yeah!

Maybe my Mom!

Nah … she'll freak!

That's when my first call came in, an illegally parked car and an hour's worth of research.

Wow!

Guess we skipped **that** scenario in training.

Phew! Done.

I was right back in service and just as I was thinking to myself, *This is a breeze* … another call came in. Did I hear that right? Convenience store armed robbery?

Wait! I am one mile away from the scene.

It was my second call of my first day and I'd only been on the street for one hour. Can someone say, "Shit magnet?"

FIGHTS ON!

CHAPTER SIX
FNG

O n the outside I projected nothing but confidence. On the inside ... I was terrified. As I pulled up to the building and looked at the numbers, I knew I had gotten the address wrong. Part of the testing process, after the regular academy, was the agency specific academy—post academy. I failed the first test question. I knew I had guessed it wrong.

Damn it!

I had transposed two numbers on the address to my assigned precinct. In those days, folks could get fired for such an infraction and I was already on razor's edge.

Stupid reloads.

I started my first day with a lost look on my face. I was immediately directed to the briefing room by the all-knowing desk aide. Inside the briefing room were my future squad mates, field training Officer and sergeant.

"Fucking new guy," I heard one of them say. "Is this guy gonna make it past day four?"

36

Those were the first words ever spoken to (or about) me as an Officer by another Officer. It was followed by a lot of chuckling at my expense.

Awkward!

I found out that my FTO had a kid before me, his first booter, who quit on day four of training. This poor guy decided he could not go hands-on with bad guys. They tried to talk him out of quitting, but the decision had been made. It seemed kind of silly to me, to go through all that training, including academy and not give the job more time. I figured, only the booter, himself, knew what he was prepared to do, so I absolutely respected his decision—still do.

So, there I was in my first briefing. There were the usual meet and greets, the tour of the station and then the obligatory, "This is what I expect" speech. I thought it went well. In fact, I remember thinking to myself, "I will be the same way when I have that opportunity."

Then when I gave my first answer to whatever question was being asked of me, it was naturally followed by a resounding, "Yes, sir!"

"Ok. Sit down. Let's get something straight right now," my FTO said, less than impressed with my eagerness. "You made it. You are no longer in the academy and as far as I am concerned, we are partners now. No more of this 'sir' shit. Got it?"

"Yes sir … I mean, okay then."

My FTO handed me a set of keys and said, "Go gas up the car."

He was testing me already and I failed—miserably. I hadn't paid attention to the fact that the key ring had a number imprinted on it, a number coinciding with the parking space the car was parked in.

Duh!

It took me three trips around the lot before I realized it. Most guys had trouble remembering their pin number to the gas pumps. Not me! I had that dialed in. I may not be able to find the car, but I sure can pump some fuel.

Next, it was time for gear setup and stocking said car. I did not care one bit about any of this admin stuff. I just wanted to hit the street. Preparation? Whatever let's go! My haste to bypass proper preparation was quickly and appropriately extinguished.

MY FIRST SEARCH AS A SWORN OFFICER

#6807

"Hey rook! Come search this guy."

Okay. No problem.

"Oh yeah … and you'd better double glove up."

I'm sorry. What?

Turned out our subject had decided to go swimming. No biggie, except for the fact that he was swimming in a pool he had no right to be swimming in. Apparently, he jumped the fence of an apartment complex and went skinny dipping.

Great!

Then he urinated on his *own* clothes and put them back on.

Oh my god!

Ewww!

You'd think, for my sake, he would have at least jumped back in the pool for a quick rinse, but no!

Selfish bastard!

Would two pairs of gloves be enough?

First day jitters?

Gone.

CHAPTER SEVEN
Caught in the Teeth of Turmoil

An Officer got into a nasty, deadly force confrontation and we, as a recruit class, were lucky to hear it firsthand. Still wet behind the ears in the academy, I remember his story sounding a lot like a scene from the film, Lethal Weapon. That's cool shit!

Yeah?

Wait! That happened and where? Broad daylight and she tried to kill you? That shit doesn't really happen! Does it?

Am I right?

No one dares mess with us. As a rookie, I shrugged stories like that off. I mean, we are Cops. This is all about having fun, jumping fences, and thumping bad guys. Mind you, at this point, I was only six or seven weeks into my field training. I was feeling on fire. Real life danger and turmoil wasn't a consideration, not really.

Ahem! Better rethink that one, young grasshopper.

This brings me to my first big lesson as an Officer. It happened in 1999 and it led me down a path toward some pretty serious groundwork and mental preparedness for my future in police work.

MY FIRST DOGFIGHT

#6807

It was an early morning in August. I was out on the hunt—a dog call. I was free, as in no FTO, one year and ready to take on the world.

I was solo, bitches!

"Officer … Officer! We need help!"

"How can I help you, fine sir?"

"These dogs have been chasing us for 45 minutes."

Dogs? Shit! I can handle this!

No backup needed. Rabies Animal Control had already been called out and was not coming.

I got this!

I'm no stranger to dogs. I grew up with them. In my carpet days, one of my clients had a giant rottie. This lady was petrified at the thought of her dog getting loose and tearing me to pieces. Long story short, the rottie got loose and found me on the bedroom floor patching a hole. Supposedly, he hated men and me, being a man, albeit an honest-to-goodness dog-person, just assumed he wanted to play … and I was right. He found me and the next thing I knew, he was rolling on the floor while I was slapping him around like we were old buddies. Suddenly, I heard a loud scream coming from the other side of the house.

"I cannot believe it," the lady said. "How did you get him to play with you?"

"You got me, Ma'am! He just approached me and seemed to be okay. It's probably because I was already at his level."

That being said, I was fully confident in handling dogs on the street. After all, I was raised around dogs my whole life. This particular call didn't raise any red flags because it was nothing new to me or so I thought.

Did I mention? I got this.

Just as soon as I found the dog in question, I stepped out of my patrol vehicle. What I hadn't considered was that when female dogs are in heat, their male companions become quite territorial and based on this rather large dog's bad mood and aggressive behavior … that seemed to be the case. I realized this just about the same time the 150-pound pissed-off rottie sunk his teeth into my gun hand. He must have assumed I was after his woman.

Dude!

I ripped my hand away from the iron-jawed monster and spewed OC spray at his face. So, you see? I had a backup plan, of sorts. The ferocious dog was temporarily blinded, yet still moving toward me. He went head-long into the wheel of my car, which I am sure just pissed him off even more. I imagine he was saying to himself, "Where are you at, you skinny little milk bone?" It was a game of ring-around-the-rosy, the two of us dancing around my car. It didn't take him long to get on my heels and find an opening for attack. In a virtual panic, I turned and took one shot from 12 feet away, hitting the giant, charging, snarling and lunging beast. It was a head shot—one and done. Although I was 10 feet tall, solo, and ready to take on the world, panic began to set in as I radioed it in.

"Ummm ... 998! Officer involved shooting?"

Yes. I was forced to shoot a dog. Putting out a 998 was not standard protocol for dispatching dogs or animals. Let's just say, even though I have been commended for my actions, I have yet to live that one down.

"Man, I never saw anyone draw so fast," a witness exclaimed.

"You're not kidding! That dog was hell-bent on killing me!"

Though not your typical call, there were a few hard lessons learned.

Lesson One: Calls can quickly go to shit.

Lesson Two: Even though it was a small event, I, as an Officer, am in charge of the call and it is up to me to put a stop to it. Yeah. It was just a dog. No biggie. Am I right?

Right.

However, it was still real life … real danger. And there was a very *real* syringe at the emergency room to clean out the bite wound and, of course, the *very real* rabies shot. Thanks again to the Nurse who gouged me with the giant needle.

Write me a ticket will ya! I've never even met you before!

Jeez!

In all seriousness … how bad could this dog call have been? Well, imagine the mom running with her baby stroller, the little kids playing in the park where it all began or the Rabies Animal Control Officer with a snare and no gun. I shudder to think. Even with a plan in place, I was far behind the curve. Despite the somewhat successful outcome, I never expected this, which brings me to the final lesson.

Lesson Three: It is best to plan for the unknown because you never know what fight awaits you next. Oh, yeah! And, as if the dog bite wasn't bad enough, the dog's owner filed a complaint against me, threatening to sue. The complaint sounded a little something like, "My dog is a champion breeder! He does the laundry, drives the kids to school and your Officer murdered him in cold blood!"

"Okay, sir, but you're looking at a felony for aggravated assault on a Police Officer, plus public endangerment … another bookable offense."

"Okay then … never mind!" the dog owner said, backing down.

Yeah! I thought so.

CHAPTER EIGHT
Show 'Em Your Gun

When I graduated the academy, I became a part of a "test case." A couple of the precincts decided to train some of the newbies on first shift as opposed to the normal and much busier second shift. I was totally fine with that. I always believed that a criminal who committed crimes during the day could care less who was watching and, in some small way, that made them more dangerous. My original FTO had gone on vacation, which left me with another Officer for a spell. Personally, I thought this substitution had more to do with the fact that my original FTO could not take me for more than a few weeks at a time. I was a handful to train.

My new FTO was *anything* but new. He was a good guy, crazy as can be and probably as old as my great, great, great grandfather's father. He did not take shit from anyone. It didn't matter if you were young, old, a Cop, the brass, a chief ... he did not care who you were, and everyone knew it. To his credit, he was a wealth of knowledge, and everyone knew that, too.

My first experience seeing him in action included a simple shoplifter. By the time we arrived on scene as his backup, he was standing on the subject's neck, a cigarette in his primary hand and his gun in his support hand. I'm pretty sure his exact words to the shoplifter were, "I don't care if you only stole an apple. I'll blow your fucking head into the concrete if you move again."

Yeah. I kept myself squared away around him.

This early on in my career, I had not quite figured out that I was a magnet for trouble. Looking back, this next call certainly could have been a sign of things to come. It was a garden variety hot call—stolen bicycles from a local park.

Yawn.

We were close by and my new trainer, Mr. Take-No-Shit who knew next to nothing about me, was certainly curious to see if I knew how to handle myself. Again, I had only been on for a handful of weeks.

That's solo ready. Right?

Anyway, the little thieves were headed right for us. There were three of them. I was in the passenger seat. The chase was on! The assumed ringleader of the three took off first. The other two stopped almost immediately, giving up with a "deer in the headlights" look in their eyes. As we drove past, my new FTO yelled out the window, "Stay put! Don't go home! And don't go to eat! You can think about it, but don't do it!"

Or something to that effect.

I had to giggle a little. His demeanor reminded me of Jackie Gleason in Smokey and the Bandit. Wasting no time, we tore off after homeboy, the bike thief who obviously knew the area well. He pedaled like mad for a quarter mile or so before sneaking into a fenced area that was only big enough for a pedestrian or, in this case, a bicycle ... definitely *not* a patrol car! Regardless, my trainer hopped the curb, which I found pretty cool ... useless, but cool.

"Show him your gun," he demanded, as I exited the car.

Being a worm-shit, green, know-nothing booter, even I knew that pulling my gun was useless in this situation for several reasons. First of all, the *kid* was riding away from me, and it was a bicycle theft, not the crime of the century. Although I was brand-new, fresh out of the academy and ready for anything, I decided to opt out of Plan A: Drawing my weapon. Instead, I kept my gun holstered and gave chase to the kid on the stolen bike—alone. This chase in my career afforded me many lessons.

Lesson One: Criminals are stupid. If you steal a bicycle from a populated city park and run from the Cops on said bicycle, you are stupid. And if, when you realize, the Cops are actually chasing you, and you ditch the bike, so to run on foot, you are *really* stupid!

So, the kid ditched the bike and was on foot, running instead of riding. I was hot on his track, smiling because my chances dramatically improved of running him down.

Lesson Two: Secure your equipment. Being young, I had not quite figured out how to carry my flashlight and, sure enough, I dropped it a short way into the chase. Luckily, I found it later and despite it hitting the ground and bouncing no less than ten yards into the street, it came away with only scratches—small trophies/battle scars for me. Cops carry a lot of tools of the trade, and it takes some time to get used to having them on your body, especially when you're chasing or tussling with bad guys. Fortunately, these days, the equipment made for us is kind of job specific, so it is built as hardwearing as we are.

Lesson Three: Pay attention to detail, particularly what channel your portable radio is on. I chased this kid for about four blocks. When I was clearing for help, I did it on the wrong channel.

Oops!

That definitely went in my notes!

Damn it!

This kid did his level-best to outrun me and maybe he would have, except that he tried to double-back and ended up running headlong into a patrol car. Unfortunately, or fortunately, depending on how you look at it, the Officer made a wrong turn and missed him. It didn't matter because junior stopped and turned back, running right into my waiting arms.

Lesson Four: Sometimes the bad guy can lose his bladder. The kid and I struggled for control and as soon as he realized that I had him and it was "game over," he wet himself. Come on, man! I am not *that* scary! It was not much fun searching the guy after that mess, but oh well!

Lesson Five: There is joy in saying those four magic words. Along with saving the day, it is a big deal for a rookie to say to someone he has just apprehended, "You are under arrest!" It means you did your job, and you own the victory in that moment. By the end of my career, I would hand over that sense of "joy" to the junior Officer because I knew how much it meant.

Lesson Six: Pay attention to where you are at all times. In this case, I had no clue. It was by the grace of God that I landed in the front yard of a corner house. Despite my clearing on the wrong channel earlier in the chase, I radioed my location. I felt an overwhelming sense of joy in getting backup Officers on scene. Hearing the screaming sirens, the screeching tires and smelling brakes burning was totally amazing! Is this all for me? It was a proud moment, even if it was *just* a stolen bike. In the end, I did what I had to do to win, and I did it without showing my gun. These were baby steps, all in preparation for a long, prosperous career.

CHAPTER NINE
Live to Fight Another Day

It was a warm, sunny day in May when my FTO smiled and said, "We need to get you into a pursuit ... see how you do." I was thinking, *Hell yeah! Let's go right now!*

Careful, Grasshopper! It'll happen soon enough. And it did because (BAM!) the very next day a truck was stolen in a robbery.

Let's rock n roll!

I was driving, controlling the radio, and thinking to myself, *Hell yeah! I'm ready for this!*

Lights on!

Wait! He's not stopping.

Okay then! Siren on!

He's still not stopping.

Wait! He jumped the curb and blew a light and almost crashed?

But ... I am the Police!

I had lights, sirens, ***and*** a badge.

He had better stop!

51

He was not stopping. Don't they call that "contempt of Cop" or something?

Oh man! Guess what! We are not at the driving track.

It is up to me, Mr. Badge-Carrying-Ready-for-Action-Six-Week-Superstar, to control this situation. I suddenly felt like the panicked, expectant father in the delivery room.

Breathe!

Go! Go! Go, Rookie!

Shit! What do I do? Can I jump the curb, too?

This is really happening, right?

No time to think!

Go. Go. Go.

Suddenly multiple agencies were involved. There were helicopters, K9s and Cops everywhere! It was a chase that spanned three cities.

Yeah! Adrenaline rush.

We found our guy in a mobile home. Well, my FTO found him. I, however, failed on the "attention to detail" portion of this test—something I never did again.

CHECK THE SHOWER NEXT TIME!

Fight was on—a damned good fight! We wrestled him out of the shower and onto the floor. It was a good long scrap in a miniature-sized hallway designed for a small child to pass through, not three grown men fighting to gain control. I was so full of adrenaline and excitement I could barely contain myself. It's funny, the stuff that goes through your mind during these critical incidents. As I'm strong-arming this guy, I'm thinking to myself, *I am actually getting paid for this?*

After the adrenaline wore off, just before the realization sunk in that I would have to clean up that mess, I had one thought that stopped me in my tracks. It woke me up at night for several weeks following that incident. It even crowded my mind during daylight hours. What if I had **lost** that fight? What were the potential consequences?

     A. Lose my job

     B. Face the shame of being beat down and injured

     C. Lose my life or, worse yet, cost my partner his

     D. All of the above

Unacceptable!

No. No way.

I knew I would **never** survive this career if I began to doubt myself. That was my first real encounter with mental preparation—beyond academy-level stuff and certainly beyond the bullshit of getting hired.

No!

This was the **stuff of survival**! And at this early stage of my career, it was simply about surviving the *actual* fight. Who could have known that much later in my career the odds would stack up against me, so much higher than I could have ever imagined? That's when I began paying close attention to the details. At 140 pounds, my academy graduation weight, I did not have a big 'S' sewn on my chest. I was no Bruce Lee, John Wick or Chris Kyle. I knew this. However, I also knew that I would *never* lose a fight. It sounds kind of arrogant, but not even. Survival truly is a **mental state-of-mind**, an air of confidence that accomplishes a couple of things. It allows you, at least it did for me, to slow things down and assess. And when the opportunity affords itself, your will to survive will take over and remind you that losing is not an option. Let me say that again. **Losing is *not* an option**. And with more time and experience, you will realize that, sometimes, there are other ways to gain control.

FOUR WAYS TO GAIN CONTROL

1. Talk your way out, an artform every Officer must develop.

2. Fight your way out, a necessary form of physical agility—
   Ask. Tell. Make.

3. Walk away, so to determine a new way to gain control.
   (This is *not* quitting, but rather a chance to rally the troops,
   change your angle or determine another course of action).

4. Shoot your way out, a last resort. Unfortunately, this is very common in this profession we have chosen.

Keep in mind, this is the initial "in the moment" fight, the physical portion. And this is not the be-all and end-all of law enforcement tactics when dealing with bad guys. These are simply ideas that can lend to solving problems faced on the street every day.

Officer presence is paramount. However, let's face it, if a dude is on meth or heroin, or meth *and* heroin or whatever garden variety drug out there, your presence probably does not mean much. He, the subject, will undoubtedly, not even remember you being there at all, let alone being an authority figure. And if he or she *does* recognize you as such, the situation will often get much worse before it gets better.

Why?

It's simple. You are going to take away his or her freedom, possibly their life. This is a thinker's game. What was it Denzel Washington's character said in the film Training Day?

"This shit's chess. It ain't checkers."

That is absolutely true. A plan in place *will* save your life, so ...

➢ Think it through.

➢ Develop a plan.

> ➤ Contemplate the "what ifs," the escape routes and the abstract possibilities that can throw you for a loop. Playing the "what if" game will absolutely save your life, possibly your career.

How many times have we heard, "Shit man! I never even thought of that," or "It came from out of nowhere," or "I never even saw it coming!" The "use of force" continuum is *not* something you want to be consciously thinking about *during* a critical incident. If you talk to Officers after a critical incident, usually a gunfight, it is fascinating the things you hear them say, things like: "That's not my magazine," "I didn't circle that car twice" or "I never dropped to a knee."

That's subconscious-thinking at work and *that's* what video is for. That is, if you are lucky enough to have it. Then it hits you, "Oh my God! I didn't even realize I did that!"

Why is that?

Repetitious training. That's what that is! Remember the 3,500 times you practiced drawing your weapon? Well, you will do what you trained over and over again to do—tried and true!

Yeah! No kidding.

We all know that, but *why* can't you remember?

If you are on a tactical team and you train regularly, whether daily or weekly, your memory is typically sharper than if you happen to deploy those tactics every so often in real life. However, for the average patrol Officer, SRO or other detail that has annual-type training, you are less likely to recall those events. Not unlikely, just *less* likely. There are several reasons why this is so, none of which are from a shrink's standpoint, but from the Officer's. It is **basic subconscious-thinking.**

After the worst day of my life was over, it was followed by weeks of processing the scene over and over again in my mind. There were a million unanswered questions: Why did this happen? Where was I? Why can I remember this and not that?

Son of a bitch! I want answers.

Okay. Certain things are bound to be suppressed.

Fine!

I will attack that when the time comes, but short of the basic auditory exclusion, somebody please explain to me why I fired so may rifle rounds and did not hear one single shot—not one. But I could hear my brass hitting the ground. I could see and hear the glass from the bad guy's car hitting the ground. I was pretty sure I was losing my mind, and it doesn't always help to talk to someone who can give you scientific names to these types of physical phenomenon. I mean, how does that help guys like me wrap my head around what we are feeling?

WTF?!?!?

Come again! I am a Cop, not a bio-physicist, people.

Jeez!

Then someone said, "That's what your brain needed to know at that time."

Oh my goodness! That was the best answer I ever got. It was the simplest and made the most sense. Another huge lesson in mental preparedness for me was playing the "what if" game—just like it sounds.

What if the guy jumps out of his car with a knife?

What do I do?

What if I round the corner to face a guy with a rifle?

What do I do?

Are there backdrops? Can I fire from where I am standing? What are the escape routes? Where can I go? What are the likely paths of travel for the bad guy on foot *and* in a car? Cover versus concealment? Cover fire? What does policy dictate? And then there was one of my biggest pet peeves at night, the problem of being back lit. Do you have the ability to fight someone and keep an eye on the other potential threats? The possibilities are absolutely endless. Mental preparedness is the first line of defense. **PREPARE FOR THE FIGHT!**

CHAPTER TEN
Calling the Shots

D uring the hiring process, and surely in the academy, recruits are given a handful of scenarios that are designed to make them uncomfortable, to see if they can determine the right course of action. The most common, as far as I know, is the 11:00 p.m. traffic stop—a stop sign violation. Come to find, it's your Mom behind the wheel and she's been consuming alcohol.

What do you do?

Obviously, the point of this puzzle is to prepare you for when *that* type of scenario happens in real life and believe me, *it will happen*! Personally, two scenarios come to mind. The first one was not a huge deal, as these things go, but the second scenario was tough.

Ugh!

The first scenario took place on a normal day in the "Hood." I was on patrol when I saw a couple of dudes "begging" to be stopped. They tried to elude me, but I found them. However, because they quickly exited the vehicle, I was unable to identify who was driving. I got one guy stopped on my own. A couple of squad mates walked up a few minutes later with the second guy. My heart sank when I realized it was my best friend's brother. Unfortunately, by now, my peers had already figured out that he had four outstanding warrants.

Why me?

I radioed my boss and ran down the scenario with him. Not necessarily to dodge my responsibility, but to (Yes! I'll say it), put the burden on him, so that I wouldn't be forced to arrest my friend's brother. It was kind of a dick move, but I was in charge, and I needed someone over my head to make the *bigger* decision. I couldn't determine who was driving. Regardless, they both ran from the Police and my buddy's brother had warrants. My boss understood and asked, "What do *you* want to do?"

"I think he needs to go," I replied.

My boss agreed, and for my sake, asked one of my squad mates to handle the paper. Pretty easy, as it turned out and as far as my buddy's brother, he apologized and admitted he needed to clear up his warrants. That made things slightly easier, but not so much when I had to tell my best friend what had happened.

The second scenario is one I wish I could erase from my memory. It was 10: 30 p.m. on a weeknight. There were two cars on the road: Me, in a fully marked patrol car, and the drunk who flew past me, driving at least 20 mph over the speed limit. It was nighttime, but the road was well-lit. I made the stop. The driver immediately admitted to drinking and it just got worse from there. The driver, a local firefighter, had his six-year-old in the car *and* he had two prior convictions for driving under the influence *and* he was on double secret probation from his department, *and* he was just six months away from his 20-year service anniversary and a full pension.

Yeah. I could not dream up a worse scenario.

This one was not going to just go away. I wanted to ask how many times he'd gotten lucky and why he was at it *again* ... with his child in the car! ***SOME WILL NEVER LEARN.*** That was a tough trial, but at least he and (more importantly) his child are both alive today.

CHAPTER ELEVEN
Run and Gun

I n the middle of July 2000, a good buddy of mine joined me as my first civilian ride-along passenger. He rode with me four times in my 20-year career. It was his dream to join the Police force and I was only too happy to take him along for a ride.

Sweet! Let's go have some fun.

Did I say fun? Actually, his first ride with me was a little more fun than either one of us had bargained for. It was 0600 hours on a Saturday morning. We hit the street and started our day of crime-fighting.

Boring.

We ended up making a silly arrest and, so, off to the jail we went. Bad timing, as it turned out because a squad mate of mine had gotten into a gnarly fight with a naked guy who was high on PCP. It would have been a great opportunity to let my buddy witness the potential of what he might encounter on the job—naked, sweaty, high on drugs and out of control.

Yeah, baby!

I could have played the "FTO" and made *him* search the naked dude, but it was not to be. I guess it would have been a moot point, since he was in his birthday suit—the bad guy, not my buddy!

The Officer involved was quite proud of herself, having helped put the beat-down on "naked guy." Being that she was a so-called "white cloud," meaning no trouble ever found her, it would have been a chance for me to see her in action. I, being the "black cloud," the one *always* finding trouble, said to her, "Don't worry. The big one is coming later." *That* remark almost cost me a session in time out.

Be careful what you wish for in this profession. The call, the "big one," started in another precinct. There was a report of a stolen vehicle that gave chase. It was a situation that simply got too dangerous, so the pursuing Officer backed off. We never got the relay info on this happening. It wouldn't have mattered. It was just about 11:45 hours. My passenger and I had a junk food fiesta on board from the local convenience store. Neither of us was particularly interested in sitting down and eating a real meal.

God forbid, we miss something. Right?

Emergency traffic—hit and run.

Damn it!

I *hate* accidents. Silly motors don't work weekends and I knew I'd get stuck cleaning up the mess. Well, we were only half of a mile away, so the least I could do was switch over and listen. We were heading that direction when the Dispatcher cleared a second time, saying that the subject was last seen running with a gun in hand. Now *that* I could handle!

Ease it up there, kid!

"Let's go man," my buddy hollered.

It was lights and sirens, and we are on scene in 60 seconds.

"Everyone okay?"

"Yes, Officer! He took off that way. He's got a gun!"

A dozen excited citizens pointed in the direction of an industrial area. I was thinking to myself, *Calm down, my peeps! The wannabe caped crusader is here to save the day!* To this day, I do not know how the bad guy got out of that car—a two-door sedan, American-made something or other that he rammed underneath the trailer of a semi. Somehow this guy was able to emerge from the wreckage and bolt on foot. How did he not lop his head right off?

Oh yeah. Damn that Murphy!

Knowing that I was much better at tracking than I was at accident reconstruction *and* our subject was running loose in the neighborhood with a gun, **the pursuit was the priority** and so off we went.

We pulled into a nearby shopping center. I believed this would most likely be his path of travel and it was a good guess. He had run into one of the stores and when he saw me coming for him, he ran out the back. I hadn't seen him yet, but the storeowner did.

"He ran out the back," he screamed, as we exited the patrol car. "He ran out the back!"

Okay! Okay! I'm on it!

We stormed through the front door of the store, my civilian passenger in tow. He was unarmed, of course, and had no protective vest.

Not to worry. He signed the liability waiver.

It was a straight shot out the back door and there he was, someone matching the description of our bad guy, standing like a statue, waiting for me—facing away.

Dude, you are making this too easy!

I was 15 feet outside the back door. I was already making my "Urlacher" plan to dump this guy. We were in a back-alley brick structures encompassing an industrial area with one driveway separating two buildings. Sound carried and I heard all about it later. That's when I heard a loud shriek of panic, "He's in my car! He's in my car!"

I moved away from the first guy fitting the description and headed toward the parked car and, sure enough, there was our bad guy sitting in the driver's seat, a bench seat as I would soon discover. It was broad daylight. I was in full uniform, and he was looking directly at me. The car door was closed, and the window cracked about an inch. He had a throwing knife in his left hand. In my estimation, it **had** to have been at least three feet long. Okay! So, it was really only about eight inches long, but still! This guy had done this before. He knew if he could crack the column of this car, he could manipulate the ignition. And he was getting close. With that in mind, let's quickly recap:

> ➤ The last time radio heard from me, I was rolling on scene.
>
> ➤ My civilian passenger was 50 yards away working traffic control—safest place for him.
>
> ➤ My car was parked on the opposite side of the building.
>
> ➤ I was facing a suspect armed with a knife and, more than likely, a gun too.

This was definitely not like shooting a dog. There was no time to think—switch to autopilot.

What are my options?

I could open the door.

Yeah, but he is armed.

Nix that idea.

I could go get my car and block him in.

Yeah, but do I have time for that?

No.

I could yell and scream and scare him into giving up.

Not going to happen.

Got anymore bright ideas?

I could walk up to the window and make my presence known. No doubt he knows I'm here.

Yes! That's it.

As I approached the driver's side window, I gave a couple of simple, but stern commands, **"Get out of the car!"**

Nothing.

Damn it!

He was still fiddling with the column.

So, the "get out of the car" thing did not work. I have seen this tactic used before, Officers shouting the same verbal command 62 times and hmmm … no go. That said, the suspect in question was still in the car, attempting a getaway, unmoved by my authority.

Well … I gave him three chances.

He was getting closer to starting the car. It was time to up the use of force. **Kick in the window**! Having the presence of mind and not wanting to shoot off my toe, I kicked with my support side foot.

Fail.

Retreat and go back for round two.

Fail.

Damn it!

Once more and this time make it count!

Switching to my primary foot, I leaned back into the car parked behind me for leverage.

BAM!

The window shattered, causing the diversion I was hoping for.

Yeah right!

I had no clue what my "plan" was, but it worked, nonetheless. Glass flew into the bad guy's face. Tossing the knife, he reached onto the bench seat and grabbed a gun, a weapon I had *not* seen up until that point.

Ummm … wait now!

The suspect raised the gun.

I'm serious! That's not funny.

"Put it down!"

I really mean it this time!

There was barely 0.2 of a second to react.

It's go-time!

Two rounds were fired from my service weapon. One shot pierced the car door, and one shot went into his arm and straight through his heart. He was done. Of course, I did not know this at the time.

Fortunately, for me, he was not able to shoot back. That's not to say that his weapon wasn't fully loaded. It was. His gun, however, was a joke. He would have been better off throwing the thing at me.

"Officer involved shooting," I screamed into the airwave.

I exhaled and then waited. As it happened, only twice in my career had I been terrified. This was one of those times. It wasn't the shooting so much as it was my first order of business when the cavalry arrived moments later. Lucky for me, the aircraft was overhead, calling my position. I kind of forgot to do that.

Oops!

The first Officer on scene is, to this day, still one of my best buds. Another Officer arrived on scene, a sergeant in training. "Put your muzzle on his back," he said. "If he moves an inch, shoot him again."

"Ok. Yes, sir!"

The sergeant in training was giving me direction and running the scene quite efficiently. As for me, I was both in autopilot and panic-mode. I probably couldn't have tied my own shoes if I had to. The sergeant in training got on his knees, put his face next to the bad guy, and felt around the floorboard for more weapons, which he found. I later requested this Officer get a medal. He didn't get the medal, but he did get the office of Sheriff of a major metropolitan area years later.

Good job, sheepdog!

Following the shooting, there was a long interview with the investigators. I was still kind of panicked, in general, so I had to ask.

"Hey boss! This is my first shooting. What do you think? Is it clean or what?"

I was, of course, referring to the outcome, based on my decision to fire. The response I got from him was something like, "Eh … looks good, I guess."

For real? That is your answer?

What I didn't realize at the time was that he was speaking subliminally, using simple, safe words to keep me cool, to set me at ease.

Sneaky!

This was the first *real* experience I had of joining the forces between God and the Police department. Four days later, after having been forced to kill, I learned I had a baby on the way, the second of my tribe— another angel and, certainly, another worthy fight.

On a side and somewhat personal note, I'd like to give a shout to another close friend of mine, a now retired Police Officer who was on scene that day. When he came through the door to rescue me, I felt as safe as I could, all things considered. This would end up being just the trigger I would need for my next event.

Thanks, my friend!

As for the bad guy ... well, he was DRT (Dead Right There).

CIVILIAN RIDE ALONG #4

#6807

The second half of this story is for my buddy, the man who would not achieve his dream of becoming a Police Officer, but who still went on to greatness and who, by the way, was a bigger "shit magnet" than even me. *Disclaimer: I must share the blame here because it cannot possibly be my fault alone.*

Love you, man!

On the fourth and last ride along with my good buddy, we hopped into the patrol car in the early morning hours. Assuming the day would be nice and quiet, since the last two times he tagged along were boring as hell. I figured we were safe.

Yeah right.

I signed onto the computer and the second or third shift Officer hadn't deleted the messages from the night before. Actually, there was only one message and it read: ***Homicide suspect driving unknown car with partial plate ****.***

I got on the phone straight away. My buddy was growing

frustrated because we were still in the parking lot of the precinct, and he was ready to "crack some skulls"—operative words for later. There was zero info coming in. No one had a clue about this "message," and I was unable to reach the Officer, himself, from the night before.

Shoot!

Okay. Well, let's see if we get lucky.

Within 30 minutes of hitting the street, after reaching my area, we were on the hunt. All we had was a plate—no vehicle description, no suspect description, no nada.

Yeah! We will find this "thing" in a city of three million. Right?

I knew I should have bought a lottery ticket that morning because, larger than life, we found *the* car parked at a local, flea bag motel, one of about 359 in *that* particular area. I made several phone calls. What an adrenaline rush!

"Help! Help!" I exclaimed. "I think I found something."

It was kind of funny. From the time we found the car, information started spilling in like mad and within 45 minutes, we had it all.

Alrighty then!

The heavy hitters rolled on scene and we, being marked, were ordered to hide. I was told, "Your job is to attempt the traffic stop when he goes mobile. Got it?"

Oh yeah! We got it.

It was time to hurry up and wait. Normal "doper time" can drive you to drink. I'm talking dog years. The deal was set for 1400 hours.

Yeah! That usually meant upward of 1900 hours.

For some reason this "doper" was ready and cooperative.

Thank you, sir! I mean ..., you worthless sack of shit!

Two minutes after we got set up, the car was on the move. The tire deflation device actually worked, and the suspect was rolling, albeit slowly.

"Ok guys! He's coming out and he's all yours."

Sweet!

Before we could light him up, he was slowing down, pulling into a parking lot. He got out of the car scratching his head and checked the newly flattened tire. That's when he saw us pull in and made a sudden move for the trunk, but we were on him. The suspect bolted. He took off running. The chase was on!

There were Cops instantly all over the place. As I tackled him in front of a local fast-food joint, the fight was on. I could not help but smile at the customers sitting at the window, staring in awe. I was thinking to myself, *Hi guys! Don't worry about us. Go ahead and finish your breakfast.*

I thought I had a pretty good handle on his arm, when a guy from an unnamed federal agency, whose face I did not recognize, started screaming at my bad guy. Obviously, he saw something I did not. For us local guys, to put it nicely, it was common knowledge that the Feds tend to get away with more. Technically, the bad guy had a good chance of getting away when I let go of his arm. The Federal Agent saw him reaching for the .25 automatic tucked in his waistband, and before he could shoot and disarm him, seeing as I was standing too close for comfort, he took the barrel of his semi-automatic pistol and shoved it into the bad guy's mouth.

*Holy Mother of God! Can you do that? That is **so** cool!*

I mentioned cracking skulls earlier. Well, teeth were falling, blood was spurting, and screams were coming from a very large man like I had never heard before.

Wow!

I cannot even *imagine* what this Fed's front-sight did to the roof of this guy's mouth.

Owie!

All things considered, our bad guy deserved it. The loser literally smothered a child to death, his own flesh and blood to avoid capture on a warrant.

Yeah! How many teeth did you lose, fucker!?!?

I could never have gotten away with that. It is not advised. In fact, in today's world, it is highly unadvised!

Choose your role models carefully!

Oh, and by the way, in the trunk of his car was a fully loaded, sawed-off shotgun that knucklehead was planning to use against us. I was convinced of this when we found his car keys still in the keyhole of the trunk. My ride along buddy got his money's worth that day, again, but no winning lottery ticket!

CHAPTER TWELVE
Burying a Brother

March 26, 1999 was a day I never thought could happen, not this close to home. Believe me when I say, nothing can prepare you to hear the words, "**He is gone, guys. He's gone!**" A community was devastated. A department was crushed. A squad was ruined. A family was destroyed. It had been eight years since the last, equally "**devastating**." Now there is a word that resonates, that describes the horror, the anguish, and the loss.

I was off that day. Still being a newbie, I was assigned to third shift in a different precinct area. Immediately the calls came in.

"Hey, man! You okay?"

"Why? What happened? You're kidding! What?"

Bullshit.

Over time I came to despise those calls. After confirming that I was okay, there was always the follow up question. "What happened and do you have any details?"

It was an introduction to evil. I realized I was facing an enemy that made me question my decision to work in law enforcement. Who on *earth* has the capacity to kill a Cop? It's like signing your own death warrant.

Right?

We *will* catch you. You *will* die for your actions, but does evil even care? I could not wrap my head around what had happened. I was not so naive to believe we, as Officers, don't get killed, but cold-blooded murder? I never accepted just how evil, evil itself, could be. I went through the motions over the next few days, trying to process and rethink my own street-level strategy, as limited as it was with just one year on. I did not have any idea how to deal with this newfound and profound loss. It did not take long though.

Naturally, I went to the funeral and had every intention of standing proudly beside my brothers and sisters to show my respect and support, even though I felt completely useless among the sea of Blue. There were almost as many tan uniforms, not to mention a huge number of ordinary citizens showing their love and support. The Chaplain spoke, then the minister and then a handful of friends. It was a blur then and even more so now, but I won't ever forget when they played the fallen Officer's favorite Van Halen song over the church loudspeakers. I burst into tears and wept for a good 10 minutes.

Why am I crying?

I never met this man … this peer … this Officer.

Officer … oh my God!

It suddenly hit me like a ton of bricks. I am a part of something extraordinary and meaningful. Looking around the room confirmed it. This is not just a career. **It is a lifestyle**, **a calling** and **a brotherhood** that reaches beyond the limits of anything I have ever been exposed to. I was suddenly filled with pride. I knew what I had accomplished and what it took to get there, but then I saw a whole new truth. As a member of this extraordinary brotherhood, this man laid down his life for his beliefs as an Officer, for his friends and for a community left mourning. What could be more honorable than that?

After that first funeral, I stood a little taller, my shoulders pulled back and my chest opened. There was a new confidence in me. It made me look at my world differently and I forever will because of that day.

Thank you, my brother!

CHAPTER THIRTEEN
The Evil Hour

I was back to first shift after almost a whole year on thirds. I had a ball working nights, but days were where it was at for me. I was two years in and having fun. It was about 0930 when the call came out—a possible shooting suspect. I knew the area well, having been a delivery driver in those parts for a couple of years and guess what! I was just one mile away.

According to dispatch, the caller gave a thorough description of the suspect, including where to find him, somewhere in the "northeast part" of the business complex. The caller agreed to standby on the phone until we arrived—basic stuff.

My plan was simple. The complex was big, so I would sneak into the southwest side of the complex and wait for backup. As it turned out, the caller did not have a good sense of direction and, so I found the suspect as I pulled into the southwest side.

Of course! Shit Magnet does it again.

The suspect *knew* his boss was calling the Police and, therefore, was waiting for us to arrive. I was full of fire, but still no cowboy. Not that I ever was, especially when going up against a possible shooting suspect.

So, there I was on scene, announcing to radio that I had arrived. Suddenly I realized that not only was the bad guy *not* where he was supposed to be, but that he had eyes on me.

What were my options?

I could drive away and hope for the best. I mean, this guy could have just killed someone, but then again, do I let him out of my sight?

Probably not.

Do I approach him alone? Well, he was likely armed, so approaching him might not be a good plan.

What did I do?

I drove past the suspect, at which time we made eye contact. I distanced myself from him about 150 yards and eventually backed into a parking space. The guy was on foot. He approached me. I was on the radio, advising dispatch of my situation and begging, "Please. Please help me!"

As he got within earshot, he stopped and asked, "Hey man! Are you looking for me?"

"No sir. I have an alarm going off over here," I said calmly. "Let me see what it is all about first."

Would you believe? He bought it. He just shrugged his shoulders and headed back in the direction of his boss. Meanwhile, the boss was pointing frantically at the suspect and giving me a look that said, "Hey man! Do not leave me here!"

As for me, I was kick-starting my heart. By the grace of God, another Officer, who would later become a mentor, arrived on scene. He was dressed in plain clothes and driving an undercover car. When the Officer saw his window of opportunity, he wrapped the bad guy up in a big, bear hug and held onto him long enough for me to come screeching up, so to help secure him. The guy did not resist and luckily, as it turned out, was secured quite easily. Sometime later I learned that his plan was to engage me, so that I would kill him—death by Cop, a very bad outcome for us both.

There were buildings filled with morning office workers on three sides, all within close proximity. On the fourth side, there was a street packed with cars—five lanes deep. Based on his actions that morning, our bad guy was ready to end it all. It would have been nice for his boss to relay that pertinent information to us

Oh well!

I guess he was dealing with his own sense of panic. It was not until I was sitting in the monitoring room at the station that I fully understood the scenario. Allegedly, the guy was going through or had recently been divorced. He was not happy with that, so he set out for revenge. He admitted to pounding on his estranged wife's front door. She refused him, and so he kicked it down. The woman immediately called 911.

Sometime later I spoke directly with the 911 operator who took that call. Sadly, she confessed to hearing the yelling between the two just before the gunshots sounded. Silence followed. The operator repeatedly asked for some sort of response. There was nothing but the helpless feeling that came with being unable to save this woman who had called in for help. Her estranged husband, the bad guy, basically executed her, picked up his shell casings and calmly left the scene. He proceeded to his place of business and promptly filled his boss in on what he had done. His boss did the right thing by calling the Police, but I suspect he did not *really* believe what he was hearing. The bad guy waited calmly until I arrived. When we secured him, we located a nine-millimeter handgun concealed in the small of his back. We also found the shells. We discussed our options, as to what to do with this guy. It was all done by the book, but I have to say our options were limited at best because:

1. He was carrying a concealed weapon, but he had a security guard card, allowing him to do so.

2. The four shell casings were incriminating, but was it enough to make an arrest?

3. We had a brief confession, but then, again, was his confession arrest-worthy?

The major problem we were having was that we had no actual information regarding a shooting taking place anywhere in the city, although we were looking into it. So, in the meantime, I had to ask our bad guy's permission to transport him to headquarters.

I know!

The things we must do as Officers, in order to protect the bad guy's rights.

Amazing!

Eventually, I got him downtown and situated upstairs in an interview room. That's when I was approached by a detective supervisor.

"What have you got, Rook?"

Now, let me preface this by saying, there were several incidents that could have potentially ended my career over the years. This one was at the top of the chart and remained so for the next 18 years.

"Well, Sir," I began. "This guy claims he killed his wife, but we have not been able to confirm anything yet. We have a gun and some spent casings. That is all so far. Radio is looking into possible shootings, and I am waiting for a callback."

"Read him his rights. See if he will talk," the detective supervisor

supervisor barked. "If he won't, send him out the front door."

Those were his actual words. I could just read the headlines and the questions that followed had I listened to him.

"So, Officer Hoyer, you had a first-degree murderer in your custody and because he decided not to speak, you let him walk?"

Well ... I think not, sir!

I *did*, in fact, read this bad guy his rights and made a feeble attempt to interrogate him, but he was not stupid. He respectfully replied, "I appreciate that you want this collar, but I need a *real* detective."

He could probably tell I was brand-new to the department and that I had no idea what the hell I was doing. So, lucky for me, the word got out and a homicide detective entered the picture.

Phew! I could finally relax.

I gave a quick brief and the detective asked me to hang out until after the interview. I got excited, that is until I realized he just needed me for a wagon. It was a bummer, but no biggie!

Sitting there, I realized how close I came to death, to a man who obviously had no hesitation to kill. I was alone with that man for close to 30 minutes on the drive downtown. It was scary when it all came to light. To this day, I am thankful he did not have it out for me. At the same time, I am sorrowful for his former loved one, someone who did not deserve to be taken from this earth without a fighting chance. Those stories were always the toughest to take.

I am reminded of another call, another "romantic" relationship gone horribly bad, this time between an 18-year-old kid with the words "Thug Life" tattooed on his body and a 30-year-old woman. Things got so bad, one night "Thug Life" showed up at this woman's home in the middle of the night. He climbed on top of her while she slept. He put a small caliber handgun to her forehead, woke her up, and pulled the trigger. Miraculously, this poor woman managed to survive. The bullet did do significant damage. This kid, in his cowardice, fled the scene, leaving her for dead. Who, but a cold-hearted thug, does that?

"Thug Life" dumped the gun somewhere nearby, which was later recovered. He lasted two days in hiding, landing in his old neighborhood where everyone knew him. We had flyers splayed citywide, including possible locations where he might show his face. It was a high-profile type of case. I did a little digging of my own. I started hanging out in the area, places I thought he may be. Now, as much as I would like to take credit for finding him on my own, I did not. We got a radio call from the local convenience store giving a full description of him. Fortunately, I was nearby and was able to get eyes on him right away. Being that "Thug Life" was pretty stupid, he didn't attempt to run when he saw us coming for him, and he had a decent chance of eluding us. So, off in cuffs he went, back to headquarters. And that time I went directly to the detective assigned to the case, avoiding the detective supervisor.

Live and learn.

I testified in court on this case, seeing the victim for the first time. All I could think was, *My God! How did she survive this?* I never felt sorry for anyone. However, I can't deny I felt the worst pain in my heart for her. The scar he left on her forehead was nothing short of grotesque. She cried when she found out that I was the Officer who apprehended her assailant. That was humbling. As for "Thug Life," he was sentenced appropriately— not by *my* standards, of course, but appropriate to the crime committed based on the law.

On a personal note, I'm not opposed to tattoos. Some are unique and cool. Others are inappropriate. Hey! It's your body.

Right?

I suppose when you want to lead a life of crime so badly that you would tattoo the words "Thug Life" to your person, you are pretty much destined for failure in that regard.

CHAPTER FOURTEEN
Roll with the Punches

Over the years, I have learned that **adrenaline is a wonderful thing**, even a tool from time to time. However, it cannot be relied upon. In the academy, we conducted three-minute drills, exercises designed to test your ability to stay in the fight. First, you were tested in the ring by yourself and then once again against three opponents. Three minutes sounded easy. I remember thinking, *It'll be a breeze!*

Ha!

In a fight, three minutes is an eternity. In this case, of course, I am talking about a closely observed event by experienced trainers in a controlled environment. As recruits, we were expected to be in top physical shape, although that was not always the case. Fast forward to the street: Assuming you work for a big agency, you will likely have plenty of backup at any given time, but what if your closest unit is 30 minutes away? There are a couple different schools of thought here:

1. If you are working for a **city agency**, you may have more help. However, do not be fooled into thinking it will save your life. Assuming the call is heard, Officers are available, *and* they arrive safely, it could and, likely will be three minutes at a minimum. It could also be a whole lot longer. So, how do you handle this? Fitness is, certainly, one way. I would rather lose a fight because my opponent was superior to me in martial arts versus, I gassed out too quickly. Of course, it does not matter because losing at all is, in my opinion, unacceptable!

2. Then there are the **outlying agencies**, an altogether different category. Because they usually aren't equipped to offer the same rapid response time as a metropolitan city, a little more cunning is necessary, not to mention more ammunition. This is a good time to get creative, tactically-speaking, because you may be on your own for some time before help arrives. For instance, verbal judo can be an effective tactic, using your words to deescalate a situation. You might consider unconventional weapons, policy-meeting type weapons. However, let's face it! Desperate times call for desperate measures. Would you rather take the suspension or risk imminent death? Sadly, in this profession, that's a

question you may have to ask yourself. The muzzle of my rifle worked quite well for occasions such as these. If all else fails, consider your escape routes, which, by the way, do not make you a coward, so long as you get *back* into the fight at the appropriate time. Running away and leaving your comrades behind?

Yeah. That's not okay!

How about running away to gain an advantage over three or more opponents? I'd say that's quite acceptable. Facing a dedicated adversary can prove deadly and can happen quite quickly, too. That rings true for virtually *any* scenario on the street, but why not at least have a tangible advantage? When I put on my public speaking events, I always ask my audience if they have ever been punched in the face on the street. Out of a crowd of 20 or 30 people, I usually get one or two hands in the air.

"Time to train," I say.

More than likely, getting clocked in the face will not kill you, but it can and probably will stun you. Having this happen for the first time when you are up against a bad guy, is *not* the time to be schooled on the art of taking a punch. I can hear the arguments now and that's good.

Yes! Bring them.

I know what you're thinking ... no one will *ever* get close enough to you to strike you in the face. Right?

I say, "Good luck with that!"

Just remember when you are on the street, there are no rules, and *anything* can happen! So, practice those defensive tactics—often. This topic brings to mind a great line from the movie Road House, a favorite of mine. Patrick Swayze's character says, "Those who go looking for trouble are not usually much of a problem for someone who's ready for them."

Be ready, folks! If you take that punch, let it fuel you. Plan it out in advance. Play it repeatedly in your mind. I mentioned the advantage of adrenaline earlier. Adrenaline is great, but it will not *always* be enough. I have always thought that if the bad guy had enough courage (or stupidity) to punch a Cop in the face, he or she needs to be prepared for payback. Not that I was punched in the face a lot, but it *did* happen, and I can promise you … the bad guy got his.

When this happens, let your bad guy know that they have screwed up. I always counter-attacked with major force, being careful not to do serious damage. However, there are those times when your temper *will* get the best of you. In that case, remember this: No cuffs, no rules-ish. **After your assailant is down or the handcuffs are applied, the fight is over.**

You see my point?

You want to give this individual a reason to pause, so that the next time he or she is confrontational with the Police, they think back to how many teeth were lost or how many days were spent recovering in the hospital or, in one case, how it sucked to never be able to throw a ball again because of the bite of a K9—story for later. And yes! Sadly, there are some "ladies" who get into scraps with Cops, too. Sorry, ladies, but what is good for the goose is good for the gander.

There were three statements I always offered before the "beating," time permitting and other factors being equal.

1. Please stop

2. Stop it now

3. I am not telling you again

Then (**BAM**!) Strikes were thrown. I always preferred the forearm to the temple method. It was a real attention-getter. There were things I enjoyed about proving my point, like watching a guy's eyeballs bounce from side-to-side like pin balls against the inside walls of his skull. I always *knew* I had made my point when that happened, which was usually great because after they'd come to, I would often receive an apology or the question, "Why did you have to hit me with the Louisville slugger?"

Ummm ... let me see. How many chances did I give you?

Keep in mind, once the chase is over and the "beating" stops—**stop**. You won. The bad guy is likely going to the hospital or to jail or both. You won!

When that happened, I always took the first step in making amends. It went something like, "Hey, man! Sorry for the beat-down, but you understand *why* I did it ... right?" Sometimes they would agree, but more often than not it was the "Get out of my face, asshole!" response.

Also, after they were dusted off and escorted to the car, I would be as gentle as possible. Without jeopardizing my safety or theirs, I would let them see that, too. It was all about timing. I never, ever, EVER lost control of them, but I also showed that I could be compassionate and that I was not just out for blood. Once every blue moon, a subject would try and exploit my kindness. They mistook it for weakness, and they always paid dearly for it, but usually it went in my favor. With each contact I made, I reminded myself that it was not personal—until it was, but that's for another chapter. Being nice, particularly when I needed information from the bad guy, I would usually offer a Coke®, a candy bar or whatever we had on hand. You would be amazed at the transformation when treating bad guys with respect or, at the very least, with the perception of respect.

It was huge!

The long and short of it all: **Stay in shape!** The importance of physical fitness is not limited to working the street. I have seen it time and time again on both sides of the fence. An Officer leaves the street for a desk, losing all desire and/or motivation to stay in shape because it is no longer "necessary" or "required," per departmental standards.

Hey, man! That's your prerogative. However, let's just say, you're driving home from your "desk job" and you see a fellow Officer in a scuffle on the side of the road. Of course, you *will* stop to help and then you just might realize that this is a fight of a lifetime.

Damn it! Should have kept up that cardio!

I have seen Cops drive away from these types of situations. I've also seen them sit back and watch as a physical fight goes down, having done nothing to assist. It might seem far-fetched, but it does happen.

Wait! You saw me fighting this guy and you didn't stop to help? Why ... again?

I'm sorry, but in that case, you DO NOT pass GO! You DO NOT collect $200! And, oh yes, turn in your badge *right* fucking now!

Unacceptable!

CHAPTER FIFTEEN
Spitting Distance

It was just another normal day on patrol. I was minding my own business when, for no reason at all, I decided to drive through a random parking lot, one that I did not normally drive through. This tactic of unpredictability is a good habit to get into. Do not get routine-oriented, not even in your daily driving. Bad guys do notice!

Think about it: It's 1747 hours and the bad guy says to himself, "Hey! That pain in the ass Cop should be rolling by any second now."

Do you see any potential for danger here?

So, I was driving through the parking lot, when I heard the old, familiar cry, "Officer! Officer! That guy just trashed my store."

"Was he a customer?" I asked.

"No."

"What happened?"

"I don't know. He walked in and starting breaking stuff. I've never seen him before."

Hang on! Let me put on my superhero cape.

I jumped into my Crown Vic and drove toward the street. Of course, it was a one way, and the suspect was walking in the opposite direction.

"Excuse me, sir," I called out.

Yeah! That's not gonna work.

Hmmm ... I guess I'd better try something new.

"Hey, man! Come here!"

No? You do know that if the Cops have to chase you, they are bringing with them an ass-kicking. Right?

When I caught up to the suspect, I wound up having to use physical force because he spat at me.

That's not okay!

Besides people shooting at me, being spat at was my number one pet peeve on patrol. Still, I learned a lesson that day, as you will read. My backup Officer was on her way. Cuffs were on the suspect and the questioning had begun. It was not going very well since I was the one asking the questions and he was the one giving me the same response over and over, something to the effect of, "Fuck you!"

That's not very nice.

Oh well! My backup arrived and I warned her that he was a "spitter" and that she should keep her distance. And, in all fairness, I also warned the suspect on more than one occasion of the consequences of his actions.

I swear!

However, he did not heed my warnings. In fact, he tried to hit me, at least three more times. When the suspect and I saw the backup Officer exit her patrol car, things went sideways—fast! And, as I mentioned, I have my pet peeves while on patrol, so down he went, face first, no hands to brace his fall into the corner of the curb. I felt bad for about one second. Yeah! It had to have sucked.

Sorry, man! Well ... kind of.

"Ummm ... Christopher, he is *not* moving," my backup exclaimed. "Oh man! I think he's dead."

"Hey man! You ok," I asked, nudging him.

Shit!

I roll fire and call the boss. The guy was out for about 45 seconds. For me, that seemed like a ***long*** time. By the time the next wave of folks arrived, he was awake—groggy and bloody, but very much awake and suddenly *very, very* nice.

"I'm sorry I tried to spit on you, ma'am," he said. "And you, too, sir. I didn't mean it."

This was a first and maybe a last for both me and my backup.

"Clean him up and go to the hospital before you take pictures and, of course, book him," my boss barked. "Then see me in my office."

"Yes, ma'am!"

CHAPTER SIXTEEN
The Riot Act

Being a part of a specialty squad had some pretty good perks, including working dayshift and having weekends off. It meant freedom to work without being tied to the radio and not being locked into the precinct boundaries like patrol, the backbone of most departments. On the flip side, however, there were the occasional thorns in my side, like being saddled as a "hit car" for virtually every detail in the city, along with a long list of federal agencies. Another one of those "thorns" was taking part in the Tactical Response Detail—to put it more plainly, the Riot Police.

When I first got onto the Net Squad, it sounded great! The job came with a bunch of new shiny gear from helmet to boots. It was cool until it came time to train. That usually happened once a year or when a visiting VIP was in town or when we were asked to babysit the occasional senator or performer. We would train to refresh our skills and/or to get the newbies up to speed.

The uniform and gear were heavy, designed to be fire retardant.

Helmets came with face guards, but *no* ventilation. There were elbow, knee, and shin guards … not to mention the gas masks. I hated those gas masks! I literally struggled for air. There were a lot of long deployments, oftentimes defending a line with several dozen Officers holding back crowds of people that always outnumbered us by the hundreds, thousands, and even tens of thousands.

For the vast majority of my time, the powers that be avoided the "typical" riot control tactics that the outside world has become accustomed to, such as swinging sticks and fire-hosing protestors. The bad part of the "kinder and gentler" approach was that the anarchists knew they could push us for hours before some sort of peaceful resolution would incur. That usually meant protestors would simply tire themselves out after long and loud bouts of antagonizing, incurring no fight back from the Police. Defending such a line, getting screamed at or having some lunatics bang a drum in your ear for 40 minutes straight can test your patience. It surely tested mine, to say nothing of the incessant chanting over loudspeakers.

No justice!
No peace!
No racist Police!

I swear, it's been years and I still hear that chant in my sleep. As peacekeepers, it is our job to avoid the brawl that would commence, should we ever be forced to strike back. Yet, protesters don't fight by those same rules. We, the Police, are cursed at, spit on, accused of terrible things and pushed to deep, dark places where humanity no longer exists. These protesters rattle *our* cage, and yet they are the ones falling down, crying, and claiming to have been mentally and verbally abused simply because we stood in their way.

How does that work again?

We, the paid peacekeepers, are armed, trained and physically prepared to do our job, but I don't see any department faring well when it is 150 Officers versus 2,000 protesters. Of course, the department where I worked was a bit larger and a bit luckier for that matter. We had a few hundred Officers to deploy at any given time. When my fellow Officers complained about "Riot Duty," I could be counted on to remind them of their oral board interview, promising to do "whatever it took" to keep the peace. Well, this is what it takes, brother! I have pissed off more than my fair share of squad mates with *that* statement.

The good thing about law enforcement, as in life, is that every so often change happens. For instance, the brass gets old, and they are forced to "move on" (i.e., retire). It may take decades, but it does eventually happen. So, when the command staff who introduced the less violent response plan "moved on," a new command staff stepped in, reshaping, and reinvigorating how we, the Tactical Response Detail, did things. Not that "playing nice" during a riot is a bad thing, but it doesn't always get the job done. Believe me, I am grateful for those guys who "played nice" while I was on that particular detail. All in all, we avoided some major scrapes and scuffles while defending that line, but one of our first deployments with the new, improved, more appropriate mindset and training was made up of stuff that really makes Cops smile, including the non-lethal pepper ball shot to the groin of a protester heard (if not felt by half the population!) around the world. Our newly elected president was in town for a visit. This seemed to piss some people off. I will never understand the mindset of most protestors. I suppose they just need something to bitch about, not to mention the anarchists who are just looking for a fight. Tell me. Why is it you need to hide your faces? If you've got something important to say, stand proud! Let us hear what you have to say!

Yeah right!

Like I said, we had a brand-new strategy in place, a fresh line drawn in the sand. If protestors crossed it, we knew exactly what to do and we were prepared to do it. It was intense. A helicopter hovered a couple hundred feet overhead while an observer screamed to rioters over the PA. Smoke grenades and flash bangs crashed all around. The thrilling sound of pepper ball guns fired into the crowd. It was epic, especially watching the dude take that burning, hot canister right to the groin.

You lose, sucker!

It was worth the years of struggle while serving on that detail, getting gassed and having rocks and water bottles hurled at me.

Damn good fight!

CHAPTER SEVENTEEN
Train Your Sights on Success

There are countless ways to get trained up. Train at 100-percent to perform at 70-percent. That's what they, the experts, say. These are not great odds, in my opinion. So, why not add another element? **Repetition**. Let me say that again, so that it sinks in. **REPETITION.** As Law Enforcement Officers, we all attend annual training, but realistically, how much of what we learn do we apply in our day-to-day work? How much of it is lost over time or never stuck in the first place because we weren't *really* paying attention? Is there one class you have attended six times, but it just never seems to get your full attention? Is it because the instructor is someone you don't like or respect? Here is my thought on the matter: If you want to be well-rounded in this profession, **learn everything you can early on**. You don't need to be a subject matter expert on every detail of the job, but try to acquire enough information and knowledge, so that you can speak intelligently with your peers and/or the brass on just about any subject. On top of that, **find your niche and lean in**! Whatever it may be, be

the best at it. That is how guys and gals become specialized detectives or

K9 handlers or a vast array of other possible top tier type jobs. I'm saying,

train like you mean it! If you train like you fight, you are less likely

to lose, and if you have a special skill set and are able to master it, I

promise you, when the stress hits, you won't even realize you deployed it.

It'll be second nature. Also, if you specialize, you may be more likely to

take classes specific to your interests versus sitting through those classes

that you hate or that don't add value to your work. I can tell you, as an

instructor, it is frustrating to teach classes that no one is interested in.

Believe me. There are better things we instructors could be doing with our

time.

One of my major pet peeves, as an instructor, is when students act

out their death during a training scenario. All too often I'll hear a loud bang

and then someone yells, "I got shot!" The next thing you know the student

is falling down dead in scenario.

Game over!

I like to think I have a healthy sense of humor, but I **DO NOT** find

this "death scene" funny, let alone productive. It's simple ... really. **If**

you die in training, you will die on the street. That's my philosophy. Take it for what it's worth, and for God's sake, take your training seriously! Your life and the lives of others depend on it. Remember, you are going to be making life-altering decisions that will impact yourself and others daily and you won't always have the luxury of time to think it through.

You may give a guy a thousand dollars in traffic tickets. This could certainly be life-altering for the average Joe. You may take someone to jail for a domestic violence charge. This is life-altering for many folks. Taking away someone's freedom is serious business, and we earned the right to do so, but it can come with consequences. Those consequences need to be considered case-by-case. Ask yourself this question: "Do I know how much time I have to make this life-altering decision?"

Take a simple assault domestic violence, for example: The person you may be planning to arrest is asking himself the same things, "How much time do I have? Is jail time a possibility?" On top of which he/she is likely wondering, *If it comes to that, do I have an escape route?*

So, then you have to ask yourself, "Is this person planning to hurt me or, worse, take me out of the equation altogether and face prison time?"

I've seen it happen.

Now that we are clear that the possibility for such uncertain altercations exist, let's discuss the next level of force—deadly force. In which case, how long do you have to make a decision? I'll use the example that was shown to me by a friend of mine.

Imagine I am holding a regular ballpoint pen up in the air and then, without warning, I let it drop to the floor. *That* is your timeframe to make a life-altering decision. What was it? One second? Two seconds before the pen hits the floor? If your opponent is not committed, but decides to act, you may have a bit more time to negotiate. However, I would not plan on it because guess what, either way you've got a whole new fight on your hands. I have said this many times and I've heard it many times, too.

"Wait a second! It took me two seconds to kill this guy and the detectives have had this on their desk for eight months now? How hard can it be to close this case? He pulled a gun. I shot. Game over."

Believe me. The shooting is the easy part.

Closing these cases takes forever. You must consider all the hands in this pie. How about the lawyers? They have a say, too. And then there is the public, the media and eventually the family will sue because some dark-sided, arrogant leach of a lawyer will smugly say, "Hey! I can get you a hundred-grand in a wrongful death suit. All we have to do is discredit the Officer on the stand and make your kid look like a hero. Of course, I charge 60-percent, so I can sport my Brooks Brothers gear and pay for the condo. Are you going to let these power-hungry, trigger-happy Cops get away with hunting down and murdering your innocent baby? They need to be punished and I am here to help make that happen."

So, basically, you won the battle in the field, but the harsh, ugly reality of the war is only just beginning. Like the shooting, itself, this will take a hell of a mental toll. You'll need to train for this fight, too. Even though the bad guy pulled a gun on you, and you were forced to defend yourself, you will be scrutinized by people you answer to and even by those you don't. This could go on for a year or two ... maybe even more. You will be placed on administrative leave and expected to have your head shrunk, telling your side of the story no less than a hundred times. On top of which, you will have to prove yourself worthy, in order to get back out on the street. If you've spent any amount of time in this profession, this is not news to you. And I am in no way meaning to make you question your decision to serve in law enforcement, especially as it relates to a deadly force encounter. Having said that, no less than a couple of dozen of my peers have admitted to me that they will not fire their service weapon for fear of the aftermath that will inevitably follow.

Huge mistake, folks!

Simply put, it is a process, no different than most of what we do on the daily. It is nothing more than checks, balances, and approvals from all the angles. This is on the grandest scale you will ever know, but if you train properly, you *will* make the right decision and you *will* come out alive and you *will* survive the aftermath. And believe it or not, it is not all that tough. It just takes me back to what I said before, **train like you mean it—both mind and body!**

When you were issued a gun in the academy, your first thoughts were probably something to the effect of, *Cool! Free gun and free training to boot!* I doubt you thought you would ever actually have to use it. However, as a Law Enforcement Officer, you are considered a trained expert, a professional Police Officer on the street who is paid to do a job. This is a job most people cannot or *will not* do. The thing that separates you from Joe Public is that if you get drawn into a deadly force encounter, **you have the tools to win**. If you lean into your training, put your best effort into it, you will have the weapon system, the training, the awareness, and the mindset to succeed on the street.

I use the words "drawn into a deadly force encounter" because you did not execute the bad guy. His decision to engage you prompted you to protect yourself or someone else. You are trained to know the difference between a threat and a non-threat. Therefore, **never stop training, if you want to win the fight**. On the other hand, it is impossible for me to forget that despite all I knew and trained for leading up to David's death, what I knew didn't mean jack shit. We got our asses kicked that day, despite our "expertise" in the field of law enforcement. So, how do you get past that painful reminder? You find a way … **whatever it takes**!

CHAPTER EIGHTEEN
A Slap in the Face

C omplacency kills. It is just that simple, but it can also just flat-out ruin your day, too. That being said, this story is not easy for me to recall, much less share, mostly for sheer embarrassment. So, here goes nothing.

My partner and I got called to pick up a girl, a prostitute one of our undercover Officers had "made a deal" with. Oddly enough, she was in an area that was not known for "working girls." As soon as we found her, we made contact. She immediately became argumentative and was screaming at both of us. My partner was standing by, as I attempted to communicate with her, which, by the way, was not working. I tried reasoning with her, but she was not having it. Admittedly, my guard was down when out of nowhere she raised her hand and slapped me hard across the face. She hit me so hard that she knocked the shades right off my face, as well as a contact lens from one of my eyes.

Unbelievable!

Stunned, I did not see where my partner flew in from, but by the time I got my bearings, the prostitute was on the ground getting thumped.

110

It was an ugly tackle, too. When it was all said and done, she looked worse than I did, if you don't account for my pride being wounded. It was tough to explain to the guys at the precinct how I ended up with a full-on handprint etched onto the side of my face. I received endless ribbing for that little bitch-slap.

Thanks a lot, guys!

It goes to show that you've got to be ready for anything in this job.

ADDING INSULT TO INJURY
#6807

While we're on the subject of taking a slap to the face, something I learned early on in this career was to accept people's insults at face value. Depending upon the circumstances, being insulted can be somewhat entertaining because maybe, just maybe, the insults hold some truth or, more often than not, you just might be the human punching bag in that moment. There were times in my career when the insults directed at me were funny and it fueled my fire, so to speak. Other times, like when I was having a bad day, I was just not in the mood to deal with it.

I remember one evening in particular. I was backing up a buddy on a shoplifting call. I was still pretty new to the job. It was a tedious call. We found our little culprit across from the drug store in an apartment complex.

She had lifted a handful of makeup products and split. Honestly, it was hardly worth our effort, but we knew from the manager that she was a bit of a thorn in his side and did this regularly.

It was around nine or 10 o'clock on a school night when we stopped her and recovered the stolen items. She was a 14-year-old girl with the mouth of a middle-aged truck driver. As a father, I felt for her. I wondered what she was doing roaming the streets. As the backup cover Officer, I kept a close eye on both her and the situation. Yes! A 14-year-old girl gets the same brand of backup as the average adult male with a felony warrant and here's why.

As my buddy asked the girl to empty her pockets, the streetwise, little punk started handing over her stuff, but then pulled out a small pocketknife and opened the blade.

Did she actually just pull a knife on two Cops?

You're kidding, right?

My buddy instinctively went to snatch it. Dropping the knife, she bolted. At first, I was kind of shocked.

Did that really just happen?

As the junior Officer on scene, I gave chase. I caught up with her quickly. Thank goodness! Imagine if I had not been able to catch up with a teenage girl. That ribbing would have easily trumped the aforementioned bitch-slap back at the precinct. I would never have lived it down!

On her heels, I could see that we were heading for a parking lot. It was obvious she was not going to stop, and so I had two options:

1. Tackle her in the grass patch

2. Tackle her in the street

I opted for the grass patch. Being young and crafty and not wanting to thump a girl, I grabbed hold of her ponytail and forced her to the ground. When my partner arrived, I was on the ground, rolling around with this little brat, trying to get her under control. My buddy was laughing hysterically. I was like, "Dude! Help me!"

It wasn't that I couldn't secure her, but he had *me* laughing, too.

"Let go of my hair, bitch," the girl shouted.

LET GO OF MY HAIR, BITCH?!?!

Okay. WTF?

After we secured her, we were not surprised to learn that she was a runaway **with** a felony warrant. Can you guess what for?

Theft.

Shocker!

CHAPTER NINETEEN
Orange Crush

I will be the first to admit that when I was on the job, trouble just had a way of finding me. Even on those days when I'd least expect it. One day my partner and I were invited to another area for lunch. She, the proverbial "white cloud," as I commonly referred to her as, and I accepted the lunch invitation. Seeing as nothing super dangerous ever happened when she was on duty, I figured I was safe, as had been proven every other time we had ridden together. Besides that, the area we were in was a lot slower than the area I usually worked.

I had a nice, big salad for lunch that day with all the fixings, heavy on the dressing. Not more than five minutes after we finished up, we received a report of an "occupied stolen." Nothing big here, except for the fact that the Officer calling it was a sergeant.

This means we all go!

White Cloud and I were less than one mile away and the "occupied stolen" was headed right for us.

*Even when I leave my stinking area, I **still** can't avoid crime!*

I was driving, so I pulled off the main drag and waited. The driver of the stolen vehicle saw the long parade of patrol cars coming for him and decided it was time to break. He and the passenger jumped out of the vehicle. I watched as the entire fleet of Police Officers chased after the passenger. I can only assume it was because the sergeant went after him.

No matter. I, and one other Officer, jumped out of our patrol cars and gave chase to the driver—one of my longest foot pursuits ever! We hounded him through several streets. I lost count of how many fences we jumped. At one point, we, including our bad guy, were out of breath and walking.

Sad, but true.

That's when I saw my chance. I went hands on just as he was entering a yard through a side gate. We had a grip on him, but could not secure him. Recalling a technique that I learned in my brutal academy training, I busted out the trusty Oleoresin Capsicum spray and unloaded on him.

If you are going to make me run, dude, you are getting some love!

Of course, the bad part about OC is that it is an aerosol spray. It hits the body in liquid form, but not without first polluting the surrounding air with a miserable, immobilizing mist, which my fellow Officer and I had to run through to get our guy. I was not savvy enough to hold my breath, but instead took a giant gulp of the nasty, burning junk, delivering it straight to my lungs, on top of which, the bad guy became *quite* pissed and, suddenly, super slippery. The fight was on!

I will say this for "Murphy;" once in a blue moon he comes to *our* rescue. It just so happened that the neighbor next door to where the tussle was taking place was the sister of an off-duty Police Officer who happened to be visiting.

Yah for us!

He jumped into the scuffle and that made all the difference in defeating this guy. It still took some serious effort from all three of us to secure him. Mind you, I could not see. I could not breathe. I could barely hold onto our bad guy because he was as slippery as an eel, not to mention covered in the awful orange substance that was causing all the physical problems. Finally, after what seemed like forever, our guy was secured. As soon as he was in the patrol car, I started heaving.

It was bad!

Considering the lung burn from running ***and*** fighting, combined with the giant salad, the heavy dressing, and the OC spray … I was done! I was struggling to breathe, so in a panic I quickly began to disrobe.

For real!

I tore off my vest, my shirt, and my gun belt. I had turned a terrible shade of green and orange, so someone called for fire. When fire rolled up on scene, firefighters saw me on the ground surrounded by Cops, a skinny, little tweaker-looking dude gasping for air like a fish out of water.

One of the firefighters asked, "Why'd you run?"

Feeling a bit incensed, on top of everything else and forgetting I had ripped off my uniform, I responded with, "I'm a Police Officer, asshole!"

I was quickly transported to the emergency room to be flushed like a radiator. I was given saline-lined oxygen and an IV drip. After a couple of hours, I was back to good. God, I hate OC, but I still love a good salad!

CHAPTER TWENTY
Rifle Approach

In late 2000, I was offered a spot in rifle school. After the horrific events of the North Hollywood shootout on February 28, 1997, between two heavily armed bank robbers and members of the LAPD, the law enforcement community recognized the usefulness of long guns on the street. It was long overdue if you ask me. That 44-minute gunfight was historical, even for Los Angeles. A lot of lessons were learned.

After some research, I worried about the possibility of an event of that magnitude happening in *our* town. So, one year, while on vacation in California, I made a point to visit the scene where 12 Police Officers and eight civilians were severely injured. Miraculously, no one died that day, except for the two bank robbers. As a Law Enforcement Officer, I must admit it was fascinating—tragic, but fascinating. There was a lot to learn. I spent an hour or so just combing through the street, looking at the existing bullet holes and strikes that seemed endless.

I was still new on the force and my concern, at the time, was that I did not have the experience to deploy that kind of firepower. The fact was it scared me. I was ignorant of such capabilities—the rifle's and my own. It was not my finest moment or decision, but I chose to forego rifle school, and, at the time, I was able to live with that decision.

Ten years later, I was sent to a new squad and precinct. Shortly after arriving, being third senior Officer, I was offered a rifle ... again. I jumped on the opportunity, as I was much more confident in my capabilities. The original rifle course was 40 hours. However, for me, it was almost double that. It took me 70 hours of training and then it was finally time to go play. Here is a valuable tip I learned: If you are insistent on downing a delicious Monster® energy drink, make sure you do it *after* you qualify or, if you must do it beforehand, eat something to balance out the high concentration of caffeine.

Trust me on this one.

On day four of my training, I had a qual. It was the first thing we did that morning. For losers like me, who failed the first go round, we get a second shot. However, when the Taurine, caffeine and methane from my energy drink kicked in, I kissed my concentration goodbye—double fail. That's when I heard the words, "Come back in X number of weeks."

Dude, are you kidding me?

It was especially frustrating for me, a firearms instructor, who was in first or second place the whole week.

I suck!

Yes! I took the walk of shame, but I will say this … when I returned to that repetition training, it was go time. I breezed through it and kicked ass all week. In fact, I did well enough that I was offered a spot in the next instructor class one year later. No Monsters® *that* week!

Being the shit magnet I was, although I hadn't been labeled that in my new station *yet*, I was just waiting for trouble to find me, as it tended to do. It was my first day with my shiny new toy, a COLT 6920. She was locked and loaded in the rack.

Damn! She was sexy.

I called her Delilah.

As a rifle operator, I found myself in some weird spots, too many to list and some I would like to forget. I always liked sharing my stories with the new batch of operators. I am big on learning in the classroom or on the range, not so much in real time and, definitely not on the street. However, like me, the stubborn-types have to figure some things out for themselves. I did take something away from each deployment and was able to employ those lessons going forward. And I cannot deny, despite the usual struggles, it was a lot of fun! Well, there were deployments that sounded better in the brochure, like the time we were called in to arrest a homicide subject.

"We need rifle coverage."

Heck yeah! I am on it.

It was my first time climbing a rooftop, the perfect position facing the yard to the rear. I had my gear bag in place. Secondary Officers were on the ground. I was proned out and ready. I had a bead on the door, just waiting for the bad guy to bail out the back. I thought to myself, *Cuz, I got your ass!* Five minutes in, I realized that it was kind of hot up there.

Can we speed this up, guys?

I was lying flat on a hot, tile roof—no mat, no shade and in full uniform. This was something I was told to prepare for, but I had to experience it for myself. Being the only rifle guy and not able to take a break, no water, no nothing ... gave me a whole new respect for our snipers.

That sucked!

CHAPTER TWENTY-ONE
Show of Force

While we are on the subject of knives and weapons, our instructors in the academy do their level-best to teach recruits the basics, the bread and butter of defensive tactics. However, the vast majority of skills are mastered on the street. One such skill involves **controlling people**. Control is huge, one of the many "bread and butter" tactics Law Enforcement Officers employ on virtually *every* contact we make. This includes "**contact cover**," an extremely simple concept that accomplishes a lot. The cover Officer does exactly that—he/she covers, watching for potential threats. If done properly, contact cover keeps the person being contacted in view, as well.

As the cover Officer, I always scanned. It was a three-step process:

1. Check the bad guy

2. Scan our world

3. Repeat

This is an easy place to become complacent. You might think to yourself, *He is being cooperative. I can relax.*

Trust me when I say, **bad guys pay attention**. They watch us as much, if not more than we watch them, and they know what, if any, drugs and/or weapons they have on board. More times than not, they wait to see if we will find them. That puts law enforcement behind the curve every time. And if that's the case, now is not the time for stealth. I say,

"Speak up!"

When I was on the street, if I saw something suspicious, depending upon the situation, I would speak up. I'd say something like, "Hey, man! I see the dope in your palm. Give it up." or "We saw you dump the gun. Put your hands up!" On top of which, we'd prone them out, if possible. Signaling is another way to go. If you are fortunate enough to have a partner who is squared away, you can discuss these tactics/signals ongoing. Practice them, too. Keep it simple though. The time to remember complex signals is not during a lethal encounter. Of course, by the time a situation spins out of control, we're usually yelling anyway.

Most bad guys are not forward-thinkers, but when they are, it can spell serious trouble for us Officers on the street. There is always the threat of counter-assaults. Short of an ambush, these are possibly the most dangerous encounters. Think about it. As an Officer, you are chatting with a chud. His buddy or girlfriend diverts you and your partner's attention. In the time it takes you to turn your head, let's say one or two seconds, it's time enough for the chud to lunge at you or to draw a weapon.

Remain vigilant.

Enough said.

When it came time to deal with armed persons, I did not negotiate. If you were a bad guy armed with a gun, you got one command. That was it. After that, I closed the distance in a few different ways.

1. Through my front sight

2. In my mind's eye

3. In taking cover

4. In determining my response

In contrast to guns, Samurai swords and other sharply-edged weapons are equally dangerous. A guy with a knife, even across the distance of a room, can pose a significant threat. You might not recognize the threat right away, giving the guy ample time to come at you before you have time to draw your gun and respond to that threat.

I always gave the knife-wielding suspects a few more commands than the gun-wielding suspects before it was go-time. Of course, this is case-by-case, but let's not forget that it only takes a couple seconds for a suspect to close the gap between himself and you, the responding Officer, and it is important to note that reaction takes longer than action.

Repeatedly ordering the suspect to drop the knife may not work. If he/she has not dropped their weapon in the first few commands, I guarantee he/she will not drop it in any number of commands. The knife is likely his/her safety net and dropping it makes them vulnerable, in their tiny brains.

There is an old video clip of some Officers in the northeast part of the country who were following a bad guy with a knife. If I remember correctly, the Officer commanded the person in question to drop the knife at least 87 times.

Broski, he is not going to drop the knife!

With me, two commands were all a guy like that got. After that, I changed up completely. I started in with the verbal judo. **Sometimes a show of force gives a bad guy pause**. You might try splitting their attention. Reasoning often works, as well and if the opportunity presents itself, I say give it your best effort. If you find yourself making idol threats, that is usually a sign of trouble. Instead of using the normal, "If you don't drop it *now*, I will shoot you" threat, try using the "Look man! There are a lot of Cops here and we do not want to hurt you," approach. Get them to focus solely on you. For instance, say something like, "Hey man! Don't look at them. Focus on me." Build some rapport and trust. *Sometimes* that is your best bet.

125

Obviously, this is a raw, basic negotiation tactic, but being creative is the key. I recommend attending a SWAT negotiation class, if offered. And, if possible, when handling a scene, designate one Officer to speak to the suspect. Having several Officers screaming commands and negotiating all at once only confuses matters. It puts undue pressure on an already tense situation and prolongs an arrest. It may require some pre-planning, but it is worth it in the end. Having one designated speaker/negotiator is a good place to start, especially when Law Enforcement Officers from other agencies roll up on scene and want to play. Have discussions as a squad to let them know that you have a designated speaker.

One of my last potentially deadly force contacts happened just weeks before I retired. The call came out as an armed robbery. Someone was being held at gunpoint. Naturally, the "shit magnet" that I was, I was just a few blocks away. Despite my nearing release date, I responded without hesitation. As I rolled up on scene, I found the frantic caller first. He told me that his wife had called and told him that she and one other person were being held at gunpoint inside a car.

One thing I've learned, when gathering intel on the fly, is to limit it to three simple things:

1. Description
2. Location

3. And then move

Anything more than that, at that point, is unnecessary and takes too long and besides that, you should have already received the basic information from the Dispatcher. Next, gather a team, notify radio, and proceed directly to the threat. I have worked with Officers who prefer the longer, drawn out method of asking why and how, on top of which taking the time to validate the call. In my opinion, the why and the how are not necessary, not when time is of the essence.

*No! We need to move … **NOW!***

Am I always right? No. But, in this particular instance, I was not waiting. I grabbed my team of three and down the alley we went with a tactical plan in place. It included:

- ✓   A couple of feet off the fence on the right
- ✓   A couple of feet off the fence on the left
- ✓   Eyes up
- ✓   Ears on
- ✓   From there, it was hand signals only
- ✓   Radios down … and we are on the hunt

The fences were covered by a green tarp-type material, so it was not until we reached the open gate that we could see what we needed to see. I was first to round the corner. I saw a guy with a handgun pointed directly into a car. He was 10 to 12 yards away from where I stood. Two people (i.e., victims) were in the car, obviously in distress. They were screaming, begging for the gunman to let them go. I took about a second to assess the situation and decide. I gave the other Officers an extra second or two to get into position and then I started delivering commands.

"Police," I shouted. "Put the gun down now!"

His finger was on the trigger, and he was looking directly at me. It was decision time. Within the span of one more second, another Officer gave a second command. The bad guy directed his attention back to the innocent people in the car and then slowly lowered his weapon. Consciously, I picked the spot where I knew he would fall if I had to shoot him. At the same time, I gave the command needed to make my presence known. Unconsciously, I did not even know until I holstered my weapon that I had slacked out all the pressure on my trigger. Fortunately, he set down his gun and gave up.

Alternatively, to make his point, he could have just given me the big "F-you!" and continued being a menace. Had that been the case, how long would I have given him with his gun pointed at two innocent people and his finger on the trigger? Typical sympathetic response: If I shoot him, one of the two hostages in the car will likely be shot. Best case scenario: He turns his attention and gun to me, taking the threat off the citizens.

Game over.

The decision was his. The only thing I could do was react. That was not a great situation to be in. Looking back, I believe it was the command presence of my voice and seeing my fellow Officers alongside me that gave him the pause necessary for a positive outcome. As a Law Enforcement Officer, when controlling armed suspects, you have to ask yourself, *How long do I give this guy before I react?* This scene would have made a terrific academy scenario.

CHAPTER TWENTY-TWO
Burrito Bandito

H aving a partner with skills I did not possess was always a comfort. For example, the blonde-haired kid who could break out in fluent Spanish on scene, quieting a crowd of shocked Hispanic bystanders or the computer genius who knew how to hack his way into the squad car computer, adding internet. One of my personal favorites was the weightlifter, the muscle-bound guy who loved to inflict pain on bad guys. We all had talents and I was *not* always the one to start stuff. Sometimes I was in the passenger seat, riding shotgun.

One day my partner (the weightlifter) and I were cruising around, playing nice when the call came out: Subject threatening with a knife. We were one mile away. We found our guy on top of a food truck. ***That*** was a new one for both me and my partner. The subject was armed with a screwdriver and appeared to be forcing his way into the sunroof/air vent of the vehicle. We contacted the subject, making several requests for him to surrender himself and his weapon. He wanted nothing to do with us. Throughout my years on the street, I always found it hard to believe that bad guys weren't more apt to submit to our requests.

What were we doing wrong?

Thinking he might jump and run into the gathering crowd of people, it was game on. And, because I *knew* I would not miss, I grabbed Delilah and went forth into the zone to meet our new friend. My partner grabbed the fire extinguisher-sized pepper spray (i.e., the Crowd Pleaser, as I liked to call it), and shouted a nicely worded verbal request, demanding the subject come down off the truck.

Can you believe he did not give up?

The pepper spray was deployed, and I remember being very disappointed to find that our suspect was not detoured by it. Nor was he the least bit impressed with my rifle aimed at him. My partner and I were zero for three. Usually when guys were looking down Delilah's barrel, they immediately hollered out, "Okay! I give! I give!" Not that day. That day things got complicated.

Damn it!

Somehow the guy managed to make his way into the cab of the food truck. Not knowing whether or not he could get that behemoth moving, we needed to get inside, too. My partner did his best "Batman" move and, in one flail swoop, broke through the windshield, landing in the cab with our suspect.

Me? Not so much.

I jumped onto the basket attached to the front of the vehicle, which my partner failed to alert me was on a hinge. It was a good thing there was no one around to see me eat shit *that* time. Down I went.

Oh wait! There were people everywhere!

Keeping in mind my partner was alone in a confined space with this armed dude, with at least one weapon that we knew of, I needed to get my ass in gear and fast. I climbed back up onto the basket, diving headfirst into the front seat. Mind you, there were thousands of bits of broken glass from the windshield scattered all over the dash and on the floorboard. At that point, I had bits of glass dug into the palms of my hands and, as I would later discover, my knees.

Thanks a lot, Murphy!

Again, it was a confined space, so I tucked my long gun under the steering wheel. I turned to find my partner in the food prep area. Damnit! There was no time for Carne Asada, not that there was any to be had. The fight was on, and I do mean on!

Hoping to prevent our suspect from accidentally finding and wielding a butcher or paring knife, my partner did his level-best to create a diversion. From my perspective, the suspect looked kind of like a pin ball bouncing between my partner's chest, the door of the vehicle, the countertop, my forearm and then finally into a chokehold—of sorts. The bad guy landed on his rear end and my partner was kneeling behind him, this kid's scrawny neck wrenched in the crook of his thick arm. They were both facing me.

"Tase him, man! Tase him," my partner cried.

Okay! Okay! If you say so!

There was hardly enough distance for it to be effective, but if my partner was asking for me to tase this guy, he must have **really** needed it. It was not the best decision he ever made, but I did as he asked. Even though I hit my mark, the 21 feet of electrical wire was wadding up quickly around my partner and he, too, received the charge.

Sorry, bud!

My partner hung onto the suspect for as long as he could, but finally succumbed, letting go of our guy. Like a bat launching out of a Mason jar, the bad guy lunged forward … right into me. I did not even have time to drop the taser before he bulldozed his way past me and made a beeline for the passenger door that was two steps deep and locked up tight. Except for the shattered windshield, we were practically sealed up like a can of sardines. The kid got a death grip on the handrail, using his body weight to force open the door. That was not working and, so, he basically wedged himself into this tiny staircase that was the size of a suitcase and then the fight became mine. I assumed my partner was still cursing me out for tasing him, but I had to put that aside for a minute and determine my options.

Being six-foot-one has its advantages, especially when teamed up with a size 12 boot. Let me just say, as a Police Officer, when I got to the point of kicking a guy in the face, you could bet your last buck things had gone way wrong. No lie. I must have kicked this guy no less than ten times in the face. And I'm not talking about your "Hey, man! I need your attention," kind of kick. I'm talking about the "if my foot misses your face, it will go through the wall" kind of kick. And still he resisted.

Good grief.

My partner, having recovered from his electric shock therapy, attacked with superior force. The kid was still locked onto the handrail, not budging.

What on earth?

I've got to be honest. I do not remember how we finally secured this guy, but we did. However, it was not before radioing for help. Once our backup arrived, we were able to get junior out of the truck. We never did find the keys, so we had to climb out the same way we climbed in … through the broken windshield. I immediately sought Fire so to get the glass cleaned out of my hands and knees. Bandaged and bruised, I made my way back to my partner who was standing with our boss recounting the story. A pretty good crowd had gathered, and I told *my* version.

"Where is our guy?" I asked.

A finger pointed to this tiny little Ewok sitting on the ground.

"Where?" I asked. "Him? In the black shirt?"

No way! Not possible.

I refused to believe this guy who was all of five-foot-nothing, under a hundred pounds had given us the fight of a lifetime. Not accounting for the monster-sized meth in his system.

Despite the ruthless ribbing we received, our brothers in Blue knew that if *we* were calling for help, it had to have been a bad one. And as for the bad guy, some dumbass he worked with slipped a "Mickey" in his burrito, causing him to wig out. And, so, because he really wasn't to blame, we simply dusted him off and sent him on his way. That's the kind of fight you stomach in the hood when Mexican food goes bad.

CHAPTER TWENTY-THREE
Sweaty Circus

omestic violence calls are inherently dangerous, some of *the* most dangerous. There are so many reasons as to why, starting with the most obvious, unwanted Cops showing up on your doorstep, getting involved in your family affairs. As law enforcement, we are on someone else's turf with access to unlimited weapons. And the list goes on and on.

In my career, there were times when we would attempt to resolve domestic situations prior to taking someone to jail, if possible, because we knew nothing ever really got accomplished that way. However, there were times when we had no other choice.

I remember one night, in particular. I was working third shift in the middle of July. It was blazing hot outside, even at midnight. I got a hot call—DV (domestic violence). When we got there, we found the husband-and-wife duo going at it. It wasn't physical anymore, but they were yelling pretty good. The beauty of working thirds was that I could hear a whole lot more in the middle of the night.

Domestic calls are 50/50 by nature. That is to say that either party can be the aggressor and sometimes it is not a fair fight. This was one of those times. Picture this: Six-foot-four inches—easy, and every bit of three-hundred pounds versus five-foot-one, and one-hundred and three pounds.

He was outmatched and she was a pissed off Yeti of a female. For whatever reason, she found herself in cuffs. I do not remember why … exactly. I do remember, however, that she was not nice … not to us and *certainly* not to her husband. We separated the two, got the woman secured down the street in the tiniest of backseat holding areas in all of law enforcement … the Crown Vic. I was in the parking lot pushing paper and waiting for the wagon. The woman started yelling mean things through the open window about our mothers and other stuff.

That's alright. I can fix that.

I rolled the windows up and said, "Play nice and they go back down." Well, about five minutes later, we decided we'd better check in on her. It was really hot, and she was way too quiet. When we peeked in the back window, she was slumped over and foaming at the mouth.

This is a problem. Yeah?

We threw open the doors and called for Fire. I may have mentioned, I am not a big guy and my backup that fine evening was a bit on the short side. Together, we made up one and a half guys. Mind you; we were dealing with 300 pounds of dead weight, drenched in sweat, and plopped over on a pleather miniature-sized backseat. By the way, she was wearing a tank top, shorts, *and* a pair of handcuffs. My partner was pushing from the bottom half, and I was trying to pull from the top half.

Somebody please tell me where to grab.

(Enter the sound of circus music).

As my partner was pushing, all I could see was the top of his head on the other side of the car. He was shoving away, and I had both feet planted on the running board or lack thereof, grasping for anything … a bra strap, something!

Eeewwwww!

Whatever we were doing, it was **not** working. And then come to find she had gone commando, on top of which she was falling out of her tank top. You can imagine. Out "they" plopped, and I was freaked! The thinly stretched material of her tank top was no match for her oversized … well, you get the picture.

I do **not** remember this being a class in the academy. It took sheer force and determination and perhaps some fear to finally get her out of the car and onto the ground. She was still out cold. Let me just say, it was really a disadvantage being the junior guy on these things.

Hey, man! I am not giving her mouth-to-mouth! How about a

compromise? You put her top back on, and I will put my lips ... umm no!

No can do!

"**You** are the junior guy! So, go to it."

Wait! I hear sirens.

God bless the Fire Department! By the time I stopped dry-heaving and mustered the courage to drop to my knees to give her mouth-to-mouth, Fire rolled up and did their thing.

Thanks again, guys!

It turned out that she was fine and, as for her better half ... well, I could almost imagine their reunion outside of the jail house when he picked her up, as if he had a choice.

CHAPTER TWENTY-FOUR
Going Hands On

I really do not understand why the average tweaker gets such a rush out of stealing cars. It's not like they will get to keep said car and the chances of it having a tracking device these days is much more likely. As a Police Officer, there were many times I saw that oh-so familiar look of panic in a tweaker's eyes. That "Oh shit!" look they get when the Cops pull in behind them is priceless and it all but rules them out of the process of natural selection, seeing as they never adapt or evolve to their environment, making them better criminals.

One fine day my partner and I were cruising through the hood. We were on Georgia Street. I was riding shotgun, so technically-speaking, the "shit" that happened next cannot be blamed on me. No sooner did my partner make the statement, "I got Georgia on my mind," a kid ran a stop sign, pulling out directly in front of us. I ran the plate and, of course, I got a hit. Junior made many mistakes that day, stealing the car for starters, and then blowing a stop sign in front of the Cops. He pulled into a driveway blocked by a gate that was locked with a chain, but do you think he gave up and simply apologized? Nope.

Bad day for you, buddy! And it's about to get whole a lot worse!

The kid was on probation. He didn't want to violate, so he bailed. He leapt up onto the hood of the stolen car and hopped over the fence. I was right behind him, giving chase. My partner stayed with the car.

Junior made his way over a large fence into a field and ran along the fence line. I figured he thought I would follow suit. I did follow. However, I remained on the opposite side of the fence, inside the complex. It was a game of cat and mouse. He started making his way back over the fence about 50 yards from where he first took off. It took him a minute to accomplish this task, so I watched and waited. Once he was committed, I moved in. The fight was on! This was another of those epic fights in my career. It was not the usual "trying to escape" fight. No. This kid **wanted** to fight me. Hang on, bro! Let me stretch for a second.

Guess not!

Punches were thrown. Arms were locked onto each other's shoulders, each grappling for the advantage. The little dude overpowered me, shoving me into the side of a car. That's when I thrust my forearm against his temple, and down he went. As he quickly bounced back to his feet, he grabbed me low around the waist and we spun, once more, slamming into the side of the car. The impact of our struggle made some pretty good dents in the vehicle and the two of us hit the ground.

*Did I mention that I **hate** fighting the little dudes?*

They are scrappy as hell, they have lower center of gravity, and they seem to never run out of steam, to say nothing of the meth in this guy's system. Rolling around, neither of us was gaining any ground. He managed to squirm away and made it to the opposite side of the car. My taser was out when someone yelled loudly from the second story window.

"Officer, do want me to call 911?"

Nah! I got this!

At that point I was wondering, *Where the hell is my partner?*

There was no time to worry about that.

"Don't you fucking tase me, man!"

"Fine! I shouted. "Just give up."

No? Okay, but you asked for it.

I took aim and shot the taser. The first probe failed because of his shirt. He pulled the second probe out and made a run for it, making a beeline straight for the fence. Again, I let him commit before I let loose a barrage of kidney punches.

Damn it!

Nothing was working, but at least he couldn't finagle the fence. Then, from out of nowhere, I heard the words, "Chris! MOVE!" I did not question this. I figured I would simply do as I was told, and it was a good thing I did. Coming towards us at a full sprint was another Officer, a good buddy of mine, 220 pounds of pure athlete and I heard the most precious and sweetest sound I have ever lived to hear, the sound of air being forced out of a chud's lungs as he collapsed to the ground.

Sweet!

It still took three fresh Officers another full minute to secure this clown. And would you believe it? He tried complaining to my boss. That did not go well for him.

1. He was driving a stolen car

2. He was on probation for stealing cars

3. He ran from an Officer

4. He was on dope

5. He took on an Officer in a fight and lost

Exactly what is your complaint? Excessive force?

I don't know if our suspect heard the words "fuck you" before my sergeant slammed the door shut, but I sure did.

Thanks, boss!

The best part was returning to the scene to look for evidence, finding that the tackling Officer bowed a heavy-duty wrought iron fence.

CHAPTER TWENTY-FIVE
The Better Part of Valor

While on patrol one afternoon, I heard a fellow Officer over the radio making a traffic stop. I was right around the corner, so I backed him up. A few minutes into the stop, I was scanning my world when a citizen approached, wanting to chat. I held up my forefinger, giving the "hang on a minute" gesture. I was trying not to be rude, which is sometimes hard to do in these situations. After the stop was complete, I approached the guy. He looked rough.

"Hey, man! You remember me?" he asked.

He said it in such a way that it spurred me to put my hand over my gun.

Uh oh! This must be one of my old "fans."

"Sorry, man! I do not remember you."

"Yeah, man! You stopped me almost two years ago in my neighborhood."

Okay.

"Nope ... not ringing a bell," I replied.

"It was about ten o'clock at night. I was taking my son out for ice cream because he was sick and just needed something to cheer him up."

"Okay. Yeah! I remember now ... sure."

"Do you remember what you told me," he asked.

"No clue, bud."

In a nutshell, I saw this guy driving on the side streets. He was avoiding the main drag. I stopped him for expired plates or whatever. He was in violation to the tune of about $1,500. He was not trying to elude me or even make excuses for his driving that night. He was honest and genuine, and it dawned on me that I was in a position to help this guy out. I told him that I was not going to write him any tickets because, honestly, what was the point? He was at least $3,000 in the hole already. Writing him tickets was only going to bury him, not to mention make him hate Cops. I don't remember my exact words, but *he* certainly did.

"You said to me that writing more tickets was only taking food off of my table."

Oh yeah! So, I did.

I remember he cried that night. He told me that he had never gotten a break in his life. As it turned out, he had been on a quest to find me. He wanted to thank me, and he did that day. He even produced a handful of papers, all current and valid. He caught up on his fines, as well as got his car and driver's license squared away.

I had no idea that traffic stop would be so life-altering, but I am happy I took the time to look past the law books and offer some humanity. Those stories of gratitude are kind of rare, but they make a difference. When Cops give folks a break, they tend to want to run away from and fight with us a little less. Of course, sometimes they drive away laughing at us, too. But how can we really know? Discretion, I suppose is as William Shakespeare wrote, "the better part of valor." And it is the better part of the job.

ON THE OTHER HAND
#6807

There are times when good guys do bad things. As a Law Enforcement Officer, it is difficult knowing or even remembering that we sometimes have no discretion in some situations. Miles away, outside of our squad area, where there was no chance of getting in on the action, my partner and I decided to respond to a call.

Hey! We might get lucky.

It was an armored car robbery—shots fired. It was right up our alley. The robbery took place in a grocery store parking lot where an armored car company and a couple of guards were doing their thing. Our so-called bad guy robbed the guard at gunpoint as he was exiting the store with the money bag in hand. It was a good score, too. The suspect had methodically parked his truck close by, taking off with the cash. The guard fired a round, missing the robber by mere centimeters. The round struck the driver's seat at the seam of the window. The guard fired a second round, flattening the getaway truck's tire. Each 911 call that came in was more serious than the last. A third shot was fired, and we suddenly had a guard who had been shot down.

Oh yeah!

We kicked on lights and siren. We were *definitely* going! My partner was behind the wheel, and it was at least a 15-minute-drive to the scene. We both knew the area well, so we decided to go on a track. We were about three miles from the original scene, checking streets. The truck was found abandoned in an apartment complex, partially covered with a tarp. Obviously, the flat tire limited the bad guy's ability to make a swift escape. It turned out the third shot was the guard shooting himself in the foot while attempting to re-holster his weapon.

Oops! Finger on the frame, my brother.

It was cool out, February or March. We rolled up on a guy walking with a purpose—head down, backpack and sweating profusely. That was our first clue. We passed by him, giving each other "the look."

Yes. He needed to be checked.

We made a giant U-turn and stopped several yards behind him, assuming it was he who just shot an armed guard. He must have heard us coming, as he immediately turned towards us. On his right hip there was a holstered handgun. His hands went straight up into the air, and he readily admitted to being the one we were looking for.

"Guys, I robbed the armored car," he cried. "Please take my gun."

Okay.

I never liked disarming guys who were not properly secured. This guy's hands were up, but how long does it take to reach for a gun? One second? Two seconds? In this case, as an Officer, it comes to down to one thing … the comfort of having a partner you trust with your life.

"Turn around and get on your knees," I yelled. I always preferred the proned-out method, but with an oversized backpack it created another dilemma.

"Cross your ankles and keep your hands up."

He did exactly as we asked. His gun side was on the same side as mine.

*Did I mention that I hate (**HATE!**) disarming guys when they have full use of their hands?*

But, then again, "**sometimes we have to expose ourselves.**" I had full trust in my partner. I knew if this guy made a move, it would be fatal for him. That was a comfort, but I still do not like being downrange of potential friendly fire.

I'll stop whining.

Our subject was safely disarmed and cuffed. A notification on the radio followed with a whole lot of questions, including what, where, how and again, **what**?

"You guys found him? How?"

No matter. He was safe and secure and there was no one outstanding. As it turned out, the reason for the robbery was to aid his dying father who had no money, no health insurance and no other way to receive treatment without a pile of cash. Again, sometimes good guys do bad things. This was a classic example. And to make matters worse, our guy was a retired Marine—not just *any* Marine, a combat Marine and a specialist in weapons instructing. In other words, if he wanted to engage us, I am more than confident he would have had more than a better chance at defeating us both.

Sum-bitch!

Why did we have to find him? In cases like these, you wonder who the victims really are. And now it was a federal case.

Damn it!

In the backpack, we found a lot of cash, extra magazines, and a box of ammo. On his hip, he wore the same exact Glock .45 that I carried … with the exact same rounds, too. He was a good dude, apologizing the entire time we were with him.

"I'm sorry for putting you in this position," he said.

I felt helpless. I hated that, especially when someone is so desperate that they would resort to such extremes.

CHAPTER TWENTY-SIX
The Hit List

I made a career out of having fun. I truly enjoyed myself for several reasons. For one, I was living a life I *knew* a lot of people wanted but could never have. For that, I felt blessed! Secondly, being a Police Officer was a calling. It was more than just a word printed in bold on the back of a tee shirt. It was an ***actual*** feeling of purpose. These are honorable reasons to join this profession, but there ***are*** potential drawbacks.

One drawback, in particular, was brought to my attention one ordinary Saturday morning in the spring of 2004. I was at home doing yard work when I got a call from an investigator supervisor from the local sheriff's office. I was informed that a contract had been put out on my life by a bad guy whose path (and ego) I had crossed. I was stunned.

What does that even mean?

I remembered this guy, a local drug dealer who rode a motorcycle and liked to hang around in my newly assigned area. I was brand new to the unit. I was living the dream, working a job I could really sink my teeth into, a job I had busted my hump for. I had big plans to save the world and, so, I saw this particular drug dealer as an opportunity to clean house, so to speak. I did some surveillance on him, collected a little dirt and background information. I did all of this, so that when he and I met, he would know I wasn't bull-shitting.

Sure enough, about a month later, our paths crossed. I must admit, he was quite articulate, well-spoken, and respectful to my face. His reputation and rap sheet, however, read quite differently. I explained who I was and what my brand new "Superman" role meant for the area. It meant that **it was *my* job to protect and serve** "Metropolis," and so I made a deal with him, a pact that I felt was perfectly reasonable. Of course, I was young and naïve.

"Do me a favor, man," I said. "I am not so arrogant to believe I am going to get you to stop doing what you do. All I ask is that you respect the boundaries I have been assigned and do it somewhere else."

I could see the curiosity in his eyes, as he gave me the obligatory answer, we Law Enforcement Officers, have come to expect.

"Yes, sir! I will and thank you for letting me know."

My experience now tells me that he was actually saying, "Get the fuck away from me, so I can carry on my business!" And at the same time, he was probably thinking something a little more along the lines of, *Does this skinny little punk have what it takes?*

The part we, as Law Enforcement Officers, need to realize is that following the five minutes, two hours or, in this case, one year of chasing the bad guy, we are *not* going to *stop* them from getting into trouble, unless it results in prison or death. On the flip side, there was a certain level of respect here and so I *tried* to keep it "professional." Essentially, what I was telling this guy was, "Look, I know you are a professional bad guy, and you know *I* am a professional good guy. We each have a job to do, so let's not make this personal."

The lesson here, sometimes that is just not possible in business. And let's face it, a guy who has been smoking meth for ten years is *not* going to suddenly quit because Mr. Badge-Carrying-Finger-Pointer asked him to. Besides, if he was making a better living dealing drugs on the street, than I was as a crime-fighter, was I *really* foolish enough to believe that he would suddenly say, "You know, that Cop was right! I think I'll quit."

That's not to say that sort of epiphany *hasn't* happened, just never with me! Anyway, I got three solid arrests on this guy over the course of a year—all for dope sales. I got a couple of bonus charges on him for running from me and resisting arrest. The last arrest was outside the city limits and *almost* ended in a shooting—so much for keeping it professional. This guy later confessed that he did not want to shoot me because as much of an "asshole" as he thought I was for cutting into his business, he kind of liked me. I suppose that fondness went out the window when the judge sentenced him to 13 years.

Sorry, man! I tried to warn you.

I can't say where the "contract" information came from, but the plan was to send a guy on a motorcycle in between a couple of cars and shoot me while I was in my patrol car. Ballsy move, especially since I worked dayshift and the area was almost always quite busy. The bounty was $50,000, a luxury car, plus an undisclosed amount of meth. At first, I was insulted.

Dude, 50-grand is all I am worth?

Then it occurred to me, this guy had the means to make good on that payment and, so, I started to get nervous.

A couple weeks later, I rolled up on this guy's girlfriend while driving through my area—my area!

Don't you dare cross into my turf, young lady!

It was hardly my attitude, but I kind of felt entitled, especially since she no longer lived in that part of town. In fact, she lived with her super, rich folks 30 miles away. I had dealt with her before and, naturally, she hated my guts.

Sorry, babe! Stop dating drug dealers.

I had enough for the stop. I even had enough to arrest her, but most significantly, I had enough to tow her car. Of course, with that came the interior search and I can tell you that any stops I made within that time frame were handled with extra care and attention.

Hey! Look at that—a ledger.

Interestingly enough, the ledger had all ***my*** pertinent professional information, including the following:

> ➤ First and last name

> ➤ Serial number

> ➤ Call sign

> ➤ Squad

> ➤ Assigned beat area and boundaries

> ➤ Vehicle number

> ➤ Workdays and hours

> ➤ My boss' name and call sign

> ➤ Precinct address and phone number

"Excuse me," I inquired. "Why do you have this ledger?"

"Fuck you, you mother-fucking piece of shit pig! I hope you die!"

These are harsh words coming from a distinguished, young lady.

Sorry, but now you get to follow your boyfriend to the big house.

It was quite fortunate that there were no personal details in that ledger. Of course, this happened before eight million internet search engines had been created. Without a doubt, it solidified the plan the "drug dealer" had for me. Over time, I realized nothing was going to happen. I guess he gave up or realized I was not worth the effort or who knows what. My hope is that he finally realized the error in his life choices and let it go. However, I'm sure his girlfriend would still like to see me dead.

Again, this is one of those things to consider when going into law enforcement. You *will* make enemies on the street—guaranteed. And while most of them will not take such serious measures to come after you, there is that chance that one of them will.

CHAPTER TWENTY-SEVEN
Hot Pursuit

Eventually time runs out for us all, no one more than the professional bad guy. Unfortunately, in the world of organized crime, there is always someone willing to kill you rather than pony up the money they owe you. I never got the full story in this case, but I got the feeling some money was owed for what I assume was a border crossing entanglement, and aside from giving me one of the BEST car chases in my career, I also got an ass-chewing by a couple of criminals whose asses I saved in the process. So much for gratitude!

Once again, the call was out of my area, but I just so happened to be on the freeway when I heard the chatter. I thought to myself, *This is my kind of call!* It dispatched as a "potential kidnapping." There were few details. A fellow shit magnet of an Officer had done some background earlier that morning and was headed to the local "criminal hotel" for follow up. He cleared that he had a truck fleeing from him, headed eastbound. Luckily, I was exiting the freeway and landed right behind the truck. I got on the radio and called it, so that the other Officer could concentrate on his driving—standard protocol. The chase was on ... and I mean a good one! It was a knock-down, drag-out and get your money's worth type of chase.

Oh yeah! It's on!

We were blowing lights, headed straight into oncoming traffic. We skidded over sidewalks and pushed through parking lots—you name it. The beautiful part about these types of chases is that when a driver is as assed up as this guy was, he usually loses control rather quickly. The obvious downside is the potential collateral damage, the death or injury of an innocent victim. Luckily, that was not the case in this chase. While the driver did crash, it was into a lone ditch. The truck was disabled, and both the driver and passenger bailed.

Of course!

The normal practice for most Police Officers is **never to pass a vehicle before clearing it**. The potential for ambush is quite high here. So, as we approached the truck, we started calling out perimeter positions. We found two guys inside, both bigger than shit—bound, gagged, and basically stuffed into the extra cab of the truck. As we pulled them out and removed the bandana from the first guy's mouth, he started screaming at us.

Wait! Come again.

We just saved these guys' asses from being driven to the outskirts of town for a full blown, western-style execution and they were pissed at us. I suppose we could have dug the truck out of the ditch, shoved that bandana back in this guy's trap and let those two felons on foot go back to doing what they were doing.

Gheesh! There's not a whole lot of appreciation for us.

After searching for about an hour, we located our bad guys on foot. They got booked and I am pretty sure our ungrateful "victims" got the book thrown at them, too. All in a day's work!

CHAPTER TWENTY-EIGHT
Blind Squirrel

P rostitution, in my opinion, is a losing battle for law enforcement. We can send out decoys and pick up Johns all day long, but realistically, it accomplishes nothing more than generating numbers and promoting the place for which to show up for a good time. Let's not forget, we are talking about the world's oldest profession. My bosses, however, disagreed, which was fine because I was not usually on their good side anyway. As a paper-generating type of Cop, I kept them busy with all sorts of pursuits, uses of force and/or cluster-fucks that would generate a ton of overtime, far outside of the precinct's budget.

Sorry, guys!

One day, toward the end of my shift, I was parked on the corner, just outside of my precinct area. That's when I saw her. She was so obvious. At first, I thought, *I'll let you be.* However, being the consummate shit magnet, and growing steadily annoyed by this prostitute parading around in plain sight, I opted to engage.

I crossed to the south side of the street where my presence would be known. I got the immediate sense that she was equally annoyed with me for disrupting her business. I didn't know it, but her pimp was hiding nearby in the shadows. He was probably planning to beat her up for losing customers. Pimps aren't generally nice guys. I imagine he must have been thinking to himself, *Fuck those pigs! You'd better get busy, bitch!*

Ok, tough guy!

The next thing I knew the prostitute was boarding a city bus that was headed north. On any other day of the week, month, or year I would have said, "Good! Be on your way. I am done. Let me secure."

Not that day. Something told me to stick with her and follow through, and so that is exactly what I did. It was a short ride. She got off at the next stop. Stepping off the bus, realizing that I was hot on her trail, her ticked expression said it all, *Stupid-ass, punk-ass, worthless-ass Cop!*

If not that, it was something equally insulting. That's when I saw "homeboy" for the first time. Her pimp was looking right at me, as he waved her into his car. He motioned for her to get down. Being the crafty guy that I am, I did not stop. Instead, I drove past them, as if I had not seen either one of them. I said to myself, "I don't see you, Mr. Pimp! See ... here I go. I am driving away."

Cop tricks.

I waited to see what move he was going to make. When he made the predictable first right turn off the main drag, I flipped a U-turn and went after him. I got within a hundred yards when the driver's side door flung open at about 25 miles per hour. He bailed right there in the middle of the street. This idiot was out and running, holding up his pants with one hand and trying to manipulate his gun with the other. Now, I'm no fashion expert, but I have to send a shout out to the genius who inspired this trend. Wearing pants 27 sizes too big was a good look, especially when running from the Cops. Seriously ... ingenious!

His fashion-sense only made my job easier, as he was not able to maintain his composure, let alone his magazine. It fell hard to the ground, and he could not stop to pick it up, lest drop and trip over his pants, too. He kept running, which was probably a good thing, seeing as I was prepared for him to raise his weapon in my direction. That would have been my signal for "game on!" It was the perfect backdrop, too. It was the pimp version of Hogan's Alley, a tactical training facility designed to provide a realistic urban setting when training law enforcement. This was one of those times I had to make a choice:

A. Continue pursuing Pimp Daddy

B. Stop and secure the Ho (i.e., "young lady" in the car)

C. Put out my location

I opted for C. I put out my location. I actually did that the second I saw the girl getting *into* the car. I kept an eye on Pimp Master long enough to catch him jumping over the wall, then I made the command decision to chat with the girl.

"You better stay in the car because I will be back for you soon," I said in a commanding tone, so to imply, *Don't be stupid!* And then off I went on foot to chase after my real priority, a subject running through a neighborhood with a gun. When the cavalry arrived to rescue me (once again), the K9 handler asked, "What do you have?"

"Well, I got a guy running with a gun, but I lost him. I **had** a prostitute in the car, but she ran, too. Can you believe it?"

"That's all you got," he replied with a look of disgust on his face.

Sorry, man!

I knew what he was thinking. *You called for a K9, SWAT, a helicopter, and a four-block perimeter for ... what exactly?*

Can you say, El Sheeetoo Magneetoo?

In my mind, I knew there had to be more here.

Please, God, let there be more here!

The one thing I had on my side was my reputation. Officers from around the city knew I was accomplished when it came to finding the "good shit."

Phew!

We were on the hunt. I was with the search team to help identify our man. One hour of searching and nothing, but I did receive a call from a detective buddy of mine. He said, under no uncertain terms, "Hey, man! Make absolutely sure no one molests that car."

Alrighty!

No further information was given, but I passed the word along to radio and moved on. By the time we searched the *last* building and the *very* last doorway, I was feeling thwarted.

Man! I look really stupid right now.

That's when it happened! It's kind of hard to surprise SWAT guys, but suddenly three short-barreled rifles raised up and commands were being given. Our boy had made his way into the laundry room and was spotted hiding behind a dryer. It turned out he was good for 22 armed robberies, including one that same afternoon. He had good reason to run, and my detective buddy had good reason to want to leave the car untouched. As for our little "lady," she was identified and picked up two days later for some felony warrants.

Hey ... even a blind squirrel finds a nut from time to time!

CHAPTER TWENTY-NINE
Muffler Barbeque

S hoplifting is an epidemic and while security cameras are getting more and more sophisticated, it does not seem to keep the idiots from trying. Stealing milk and diapers for your kids … you get a pass from me, but the items some people lift just makes my head spin. One day while on duty, a young tweaker stole some sprinkler heads from the local home improvement store. Sprinkler heads?

Okay.

Thirty-bucks worth in hand and he darted out the door. Security chased after him, but soon gave up. This kid must have needed these things pretty bad, bad enough to run headlong into traffic. As it happened, I was right there. I saw the commotion just about the time the call came out. By then the kid had run through the bushes, across the sidewalk and straight into the roadway with cars buzzing along at 40 to 50 miles per hour. The curb lane was as far as he got. Because he did not look both ways before crossing, he kissed the front grill of a large sedan. He ended up underneath the muffler of the car behind the sedan, which, unfortunately, was cooking him like a sizzling slab of ribs on a barbeque grill. How he planned to "Frogger" his way across six lanes of traffic while in a dead sprint is beyond me. It was hard not to laugh at the stupidity of it all.

I'm sorry.

The kid suffered a broken ankle, a broken leg (above and below the knee), a broken hip, multiple broken ribs, and a hole in his cheek. I have no clue where that came from. It looked like someone shoved a pencil into his face. And that was just from the initial hit. Basically, the sedan ran him over, but not before bending him in half, sideways, and breaking the entire left side of his body.

Owie!

And then the car behind the sedan ran him over. The driver of the second car stopped almost immediately. All of this for 30 dollars' worth of sprinkler heads.

Wow!

As I approached the car, I heard screaming. Not from the pain of the multiple broken bones, but from the muffler that was resting directly on his bare chest. It was literally sizzling, sounding like French fries being dumped into a hot vat of grease.

Awesome!

We were able to pull him out from under the car. I watched his chest rise, not from breathing, but from his skin bubbling. He lived. He was banged up pretty good though and I can only imagine him trying to explain to the emergency room doctors what happened. Sprinkler heads, huh?

Lost that fight ... didn't you, Dumbass?

CHAPTER THIRTY
Eat and Run

When Cops want to eat; they want to eat. However, eating in restaurants while in uniform can be a gamble. Inevitably, there are the usual suspects with the unusual questions, like the dude who asks, "Hey! Can I ask you a question?" or the kid who inquires, "Do you have a badge sticker?" My favorites were the security guards who liked to speak in "code," so as if to impress us. Here's the thing, guys. The codes are usually made up and, well, the truth is, we do not care. Talk normal.

I'm sorry if anyone is feeling butt hurt right now.

Obviously, the threats against Law Enforcement Officers are potentially lethal, which is why most Officers prefer to eat in the safest places (i.e., the precinct, backed into a corner at the top floor of a parking garage, a firehouse). If we get lucky, the firefighters on duty are cooking, which could be anytime between the hours of one o'clock in the morning and one o'clock the next morning. Their kitchen is open 24/7.

Thanks, guys!

One common interruption is the radio call that happens just about the time our food arrives or when we are halfway through our meal. Either way, we end up paying for food we can't finish. Deep down we hope our squad mates will answer the call in our stead, remembering and appreciating the importance of our taking a break.

But don't count on it!

Another interruption, although rare, is the "crime in progress on the premises."

Damn you, Murphy!

And, naturally, by the time you get to *that* call it is over and done with and usually did not require our attention in the first place. It reminds me of one day when my partner and I decided to hit a local taco joint. While we were seated inside, shoving yummy Carne Asada into our necks, the manager started yelling for us.

"He is breaking into the shed!"

Damn it!

So ... out we went! The nitwit was trying to steal a ladder from behind a locked gate. Of course, the sub-genius did not see our patrol car parked in the lot.

"Hey!" my partner shouted sharply.

Caught off guard, our suspect jumped off the eight-foot shed, and the chase was on. Realistically, we didn't have much on this guy, but that didn't keep us from pursuing him across a major intersection and through a long line of moving cars … straight into a parking lot. We zigzagged around until we ended up back in the street, chasing him alongside more moving cars, at which time he switched directions and decided to cross over in front of traffic. It reminded me of the children's game of Red Rover. Now, there were times when I almost wanted to reward a guy his freedom for his effort and, had I been alone, I probably would have. However, my overzealous partner wouldn't quit.

Damn it.

I imagine getting hit by one car probably sucks, but getting hit by *two* cars must really suck. I give this guy an "A" for effort for getting hit twice by the same car.

Awesome!

And would you believe it? He was *still* on the move! He was literally up and off the ground and running again. It was a good three or four minutes into the chase when we saw him hiding halfway under a car in an apartment complex. Of course, he wouldn't just give up, and so the fight was on. Because of his awkward position beneath the car, we could not secure him by normal means. So, we deployed the taser. The probes barely got him to comply, but it was enough to gain *some* control or so I thought. My partner was on the taser, and I went hands on. That wasn't working either. We struggled for several more seconds before I remembered **the golden rule of ground fighting and that is "Control the head—control the body."**

Okay! Let me give that a try.

Hey! It worked. He was quickly cuffed, and I was back on my feet, catching my breath. My partner screamed, "We need fire!"

I spun around to look.

What happened?

I figured during our split-second altercation, he had:

A. Stabbed himself with a knife or

B. We killed him with the taser

Nope.

The answer was C, a pebble. A tiny rock on the ground made contact with his eyebrow and split him like a filet knife into the soft flesh of a fresh salmon. Blood was gushing like I had never seen blood gush. My first thought was, *How cool*! I never got one to do ***that*** before. Roll fire!

Sorry, man! You will be fine.

Thirty-four stitches later—14 internal and 20 external. It was a funny fight. The dude never did get his ladder and my partner, and I never got to finish our Carne Asada.

CHAPTER THIRTY-ONE
Firearms Instructor

O ne fine day I took a break from chasing bad guys. This was probably good for everyone. While in the indoor range at the precinct, my good buddy insisted that I shoot his Glock .45.

Sure! Why not?

Up to that point, I had only fired my Glock .40. I never even considered another caliber. ***That's*** what they issued me, so ***that's*** what I shot. My .40 did the job the first two go rounds, so why would I ...

Ooooohhh man! This thing shoots niiiiice!

It was perfect timing, as it turned out because two weeks later, I was in firearms instructor school. Naturally, I had to buy my own .45.

Right?

Well, I actually bought two of them. I mean, you got to have a backup! Yeah?

On the first day of qual, I achieved a perfect score.

First time ever!

Man, I was proud of myself! Firearms instructor school was two weeks of pure fun, shooting some of the coolest weapons EVER! I was learning a lot. Becoming an instructor for, what I believed to be, one of the *most* important skill sets we Cops *must* have. So, I got my little certificate. I proudly mounted it on my wall and the best part was that I had free access to the range whenever I wanted.

Sweet!

And believe me I took advantage of that. Free ammo and free range time?

Yeah!

Becoming a firearms instructor was good for me. As it turned out, I was good at it. On top of which, I was bettering myself as a shooter. Still, I was much more interested in teaching other Officers than I was of honing my own skills. Suddenly there was joy in offering my professional advice, as limited as it was, and having Officers take heed of it.

LOW CALIBER LESSON
#6807

About a month after I received my firearms instructor certificate, my partner and I made a traffic stop—five little gangsters in a Cadillac. Realizing that we had our hands full, my partner called for another unit.

Before long we were safe. All the gangsters were out of the car and cuffed.

Mind you, I am a certified firearms instructor, but I am not a hardcore "gun guy." In other words, I cannot tell you the latest and greatest gun on the market or talk ballistics tables or jack shit about guns. I know my fair share, but my point is that there are some handguns with locking slides and some without. The "without" locking slides is where I got into trouble that day.

While conducting a search of the Cadillac, I found a .25 auto stuffed underneath the backseat. I was gloved up. The gun was pointed in a safe direction—good backdrop and so forth. I looked for, touched and found a round in the chamber. Technically, the round was not chambered for that particular gun and since I did not know calibers well, I was not going to try and guess. So, before realizing that weapon did *not* lock back, I pulled the slide and it slipped forward, cranking off the round.

Yeah.

Oh man! There was no way to play *this* one off.

Wait! Maybe I can.

All five of our little gangsters jumped at the sound of the fire. And, yes, folks … I jumped too. When I stood up, I confidently squared up and said, "You boys see that shit? That is how we handle the guns we find down here!"

Hee! Hee!

They totally believed it, too.

Idiots!

My partner, however, not so much. He knew I was an idiot, and he was right. As for my boss, even though I could not actually see him, I knew for a fact he was shaking his head on the phone when he asked, "Didn't you just graduate from firearms instructor school?"

"Well, yes, sir! You see what happened was ..."

It was fortunate for me that I had a ***really*** understanding boss at the time. What could have ended in a suspension, of sorts, ended up on the Executive Officer Chief's desk and then trickled back down the chain of command resulting in a verbal "coaching." Lucky for me!

Thanks again, boss!

HIGH CALIBER LESSON
#6807

On a positive note, and to highlight one of my proudest moments as an instructor was when I got a request to help a fellow Officer with some mag exchange issues— normal stuff in the beginning. It was mostly, "Let me see what you are doing," type of stuff. After some observation, we went lights out. I'm talking zero ambient light.

"Are you nuts," the Officer asked.

As a matter of fact, I am.

Here's what we're going to do:

- ➤ One hour

- ➤ In the dark

- ➤ No breaks

- ➤ No shooting, just drawing from the holster and mag exchanges and then we'll go lights on

- ➤ Repeat for another ten minutes or so

- ➤ Return in two days, and then start again *with* shooting

The Officer left the training feeling better, not fully confident, but better. Fast forward a few weeks. The Officer returned and said to me, "Man, you saved my life!"

Wait. What?

I secretly loved hearing those words, though I don't take credit for actually *saving* this man's life. *He* did the work. It's not my story to tell, but the Officer did his job. There was a gunfight in the wee hours of the night. He got forced into doing a mag exchange and because of his training was able to get himself back into the fight. Besides this Officer performing at peak level, my proudest moment as an instructor was when investigators asked him why he swapped mags, he replied, "I don't even remember doing it."

Muscle memory, my friends! Muscle memory.

Good fight, Warrior! Glad you are okay.

CHAPTER THIRTY-TWO
Running Code

It was a sunny day in September 2013. I was riding marked with a new partner. We were outside of town and heading eastbound for some grub when the call came out—stolen vehicle last seen heading westbound on the freeway.

Come on, man! We will find him for sure.

We traveled about ten miles before exiting the freeway, only to get right back on, landing in the gore point … where we waited. Five seconds was all it took.

"There he is!"

"Oh no," exclaimed my partner. "Here we go again!"

He had heard all the stories and had been with me for several months, so he knew what was coming. There were a couple of undercover cars also following the vehicle. Aircraft was launching, too.

Okay. We will hang back until it is time.

We followed for several miles. Not much was happening. We had to clear the local, small airport space before the aircraft could intercept.

Our under-covers took over. Aircraft had it. Marked units stayed back, out of sight—standard-operating procedure. The plan was to follow him until he went to ground, pretty common tactic, albeit short-lived in this case.

"Okay, guys! We are clear. Light him up!"

I cannot believe he is not stopping!

"Okay," I breathed. "Settle in. Here we go."

Marked unit lit him up. The bad guy punched it to 70 miles per hour or so, by my estimate. At about a 45-degree angle, he went right into the back of a semi-trailer—not just any random semi-trailer. He strategically picked his perfect target, a tanker truck. It was stunning to witness what a one-ton truck could do with sheer force behind it. It was another one of those "had I not seen it for myself, I wouldn't have believed it" moments.

Holy Mother of God!

The truck jackknifed, sliding down the freeway. Honestly, I was just waiting for it to roll. The truck driver was heads up, as he mashed the gas pedal and righted the trailer.

Nicely done!

When we sped past the semi, the driver's eyes were the size of pie plates.

Whoa.

"Dude, get your rifle ready. We're going to shoot this guy!"

It was carnage, absolute carnage. There were two more attempts at overturning semi-trucks, on top of which there were more than 20 cars hit and/or forced off the road. We had reached open farm fields and were hauling ass eastbound. Meanwhile, coming from the south about a half-mile away was a school bus.

Four count breaths.

My adrenaline was over the top. This was the longest it *ever* took to calm myself. There were angels everywhere that day because even the bus driver was heads up, stopping just short of the intersection. That is when I decided our best move was to back off from the crowd. I remember thinking, *When this dude crashes, he is going to take five or six innocents with him.* I did not want to see that happen. I figured he would, of course, survive and take off running and my partner and I would be there to run him over. It did not quite happen that way, but he did purposely try and run down a Motor Officer who was standing *in* the roadway doing traffic control, completely unrelated to our mess. The Officer saw us coming at him and later said, "Well, I saw him [i.e., the bad guy] coming and threw my hands up to get him to stop. I'm a motor that's *all* I know how to do!"

The way he recounted that story still makes me laugh. When he realized the hand signals weren't working, he ran into the desert. From my perspective, all I remember seeing was the bottom of his boots as he dove into the dirt. Somehow his bike remained standing, despite taking a square hit from this huge truck. It *completely* destroyed the impacted side and dug the kickstand about four inches into the asphalt. The bike was totaled, but it was a narrow escape for that Motor Officer.

Wow!

Our bad guy drove a couple more miles and made a hard U-turn. We were about 35 minutes into the chase when there was a head-on collision with a patrol car—Chevy Tahoe versus a one-ton truck. It was deliberate. The bad guy was trying to engage us. The solo Officer fired his rifle from the driver's seat, through his own windshield. He had to be extricated, having been launched backward into a ditch. Two other Officers fired their handguns at our bad guy who was *still* on the move.

Meanwhile, my partner and I had stopped several hundred yards up the road. It was no man's land, wide open roadway with absolutely no cover. My partner and I readied our rifles. We had two plans in place, both identical. It was not a preplanned tactic, but it made sense to us at the time. Almost in unison, we shouted, "When he reaches that sign … he is *mine!*"

Our Tahoe was potential concealment, but after the damage we saw him inflict on other vehicles, that did **not** seem like a great option. There was nowhere to run and the only protection we had from this out-of-control lunatic were our rifles. The profound words of a fellow Officer and friend echoed in my head, "Sometimes we have to expose ourselves."

Damn it! I really hate that.

My partner was the first man out. He was one-hundred percent exposed, standing in the street about 20 feet in front of the Tahoe. A couple of seconds later, I was out, standing just outside the driver's door. I was tracking our boy, who had picked up speed and was heading our way—fast. We later estimated that he was driving somewhere between 45 and 50 miles per hour and paced off 28 yards from our shooting platforms to his door. My partner shot seven rounds right through the door of this guy's truck. About one-and-a-half seconds later, nine rounds from my rifle, my Delilah, shot straight through the same door.

It was Swiss cheese.

He was hit and decided he did **not** want to play anymore, so our bad guy coasted to a complete stop about 250 yards up the road. My partner and I quickly checked each other for bullet holes, having heard the barrage of gunfire down the road, not knowing if it was him or us shooting. Then we dashed to where the driver waited in the roadway. Surrounding the back of his vehicle, we knew we would be forced to extract him, which was a pretty significant risk. Our K9 handler formulated a quick plan. We moved up together, closing the 30-yard-distance.

Suddenly, the truck started to roll forward. Was he planning something new for us? Was he trying to get back on the gas and bolt again? It didn't much matter because we eventually got to the cab of the truck, managing to pull him out, despite his sweaty 6'6, 260-pound frame.

He is a biggin!

Oh yeah! And he was covered in blood! God bless the .223/.556 hollow point and a quick trigger finger. Just then a Police supervisor on scene *thought* it was a good idea to grab my rifle barrel to secure me. He did not like my stance over knucklehead and tried to move me. I have a couple of *major* issues here: First off, how do you know if I am squared away or not … or if I have my finger on the trigger?

Startle responses mean anything to you?

Forget the fact that I was, quite obviously, pretty assed-up. And where exactly was my muzzle pointing? It was a head shot, for sure, and at point blank range! An unintentional discharge might have been tough to explain. And, lastly, how do you know I was not going to spin around and clock you? I mean, why would I think that someone other than a bad guy would elect to grab my gun?

Okay. Point made.

Anyway … our bad guy was removed from the cab and secured with the reasonable force necessary to affect the arrest.

CHAPTER THIRTY-THREE
Emotional Chokehold

U gly topic by nature—emotions. **Emotional preparedness is third in line**, behind mental and physical. However, it is an important fight, and quite possibly, the most important of the three. Truth be told, my generation of Officers was mostly focused on financial survival and physical fitness. Combined with the kinder, gentler generation of law enforcement, it did not seem like bad things could ever happen. It's not that anyone failed us as "rookies," but I never *seriously* considered the possibility of taking part in such a horrific scene, let alone unknowingly driving back to a precinct I hadn't worked at for over a year following one of my own critical incidents. **The emotional toll was just about at its limit for me**. However, me being Super Cop, I denied the fact that anything was wrong. It's what I signed up for. Right? At least that's what people say.

Oh yeah! Be careful of that statement.

Like so many other misconceptions, the mistaken belief that it's what we Law Enforcement Officers "signed up for," is now being scrutinized, if not heavily frowned upon in our community. I admit. I've said it and, at times, I've even believed it, but at the end of the day I had to ask myself, "Did I sign up or volunteer to watch a lifeless child being pulled from an algae-green pool or to have a chud spit in my face or to watch an Officer die in the street?" Shoot! I guess the answer is no. However, I did break my back, as well as sweat and bleed and cause my family to suffer just to *wear* this badge. Was it naïve of me to believe that nothing bad could ever happen? Perhaps, but that is life. No one ever thinks anything truly bad can happen and it's not just Cops.

Unfortunately, we as Law Enforcement Officers might see more in one shift than the average person will see in a decade or ever. Why is that? Are we just crazy Type "A" personalities who get a thrill out of running toward the sound of gunfire?

I mean, who does that?

We do and surely, it's **not** for the money. The "why" is a relevant question that not even *we* have an answer for, but I will say it is a calling, a definite desire to help others. Is it for reasons of personal satisfaction? I suppose. The problem for a lot of us is keeping that drive going. Cops are cynical, jaded, untrusting machines at work and sometimes at home, too. But when did that happen? What changed in the heart of a young, eager recruit wearing a business suit in the employment services office, swearing to do "*whatever* it takes" and becoming the burned-out veteran Law Enforcement Officer saying, "My God! Twenty years cannot come soon enough!"

I'll tell you what changed. It was the reality of life in all its carnage, chaos, and devastation over the course of a career. These are the things that commonly break Law Enforcement Officers down, pushing them to seek new careers, sometimes prematurely. And then what happens? Die soon after retirement? Commit suicide? What do we do? How do we fix it? *Can* it be fixed?

I believe it can.

In my tiny brain and humble opinion, self-realization and/or simple awareness, along with admission are the key. Bottom line: Bad shit happens, and it is unlikely that we have the power to change the outcome of any given situation. On top of which, admitting to ourselves that there will be times when we just can't handle any more and, ultimately, realizing that we may never know how many lives we actually saved. What we must remember, if not prioritize in our recovery is the act of saving ourselves. If we can't save ourselves, how can we save others? And guess what, people.

IT IS OK TO SAY, "I'M NOT OKAY."

You are worth fighting for, as much as anyone else. And find something outside of your work, something that drives you. For example, one simple way for me to regain some control in my life was to step out of the Cop world on a regular basis. That is to say, do **not** discuss Cop stuff with friends on a hiking trail. Try not to recount certain events as you are water skiing or woodworking or playing the piano or just sitting around the campfire. Now, having said that, allow me to clarify.

Yes. It is okay, if not important to recount those impactful events, just not to the point where they consume you. Figure out **your** way to disengage, whatever that happens to be. For me, it was motorcycles. I ride. I always have, but I realized something about myself over the last few years. When I would ride, I would tell myself it was an "escape." On some level, I was right. It was an escape. However, it was denial, too. What was **really** happening? My bike rides were freeing me from being a Cop, but at the same time, they were putting the bad stuff on hold. I wasn't sorting through my "stuff." Instead, I would get on my motorcycle and put them out of my mind altogether, ignoring them. And when I returned from my ride, they were still there. The problem for me was that I was *burying* them, instead of facing and working through them.

So, I purposefully began to allow my brain to process the bad stuff during my rides. It was my new plan of attack to *free* myself of the daily carnage. It was only one of my many ways to escape and focus on the positives, as well as the negatives. I made conscious deductions while there was no one else around, so that I did not have to justify my actions, right or wrong, to anyone but me. And if I ever had doubts, I would make an effort to remember them and ask questions at the appropriate time to the appropriate people. There is a lot to process in this line of work and, after a handful of years of concentrated effort, I am not done yet.

Another resort for me is to find a spot where I find peace. I call these "my God moments." My number one spot is the beach, followed by the forest … anywhere I can go and reflect and stare at the world without interruption. With the exception of the occasional hornet or the blood-sucking mosquito, I have found pure peace in the sound of the waves or the whistle of the wind through the trees. Those things are very soothing.

While I am on a roll, I will briefly hit on **sleep deprivation**. For Cops, it can be an occupational hazard. Fortunately, it never caused me any major issues, but it certainly *could* have. Again, finding those "peaceful spots," more often than not, allows me to relax and sleep. Being uber-aware of my surroundings, as I am trained to be, I am pretty cautious about the remote locations I choose. If I ever hear banjos in the distance, I am out of there!

Here's an admission for you. We Cops are a pain in the ass! We can be mulish, rigid, and unforgiving, even of ourselves. Trust me. No one is harder on us than we are on ourselves. And we've all asked the question, **"How can I ask for help when I have made a career of helping others?"**

The fallacy is that asking for help makes us weak, a victim, a statistic like the people we are sworn to protect. You say, *"They* need help, not me!" Well, I'm here to tell you, if you're asking the question, chances are it's because you need the help, my brother/my sister. I can say that because it was me and, if you've worn the badge for any length of time, you're not so unlike me that you can't ask for help. Yes! Go ahead. Throw this book across the room, if it makes you feel better, but please, at some point, pick it up again and continue reading.

THE OTHER HALF OF THE BATTLE
#6807

Admitting you need help is only half the battle. The other half, sadly, is that we cannot always trust that those we report to will have our back when we come to them for help. The truth is we feel alienated, if we do not comply with the "group." I cannot fathom being teased, tormented or, worse yet, ousted because I exposed the emotional chink in my armor brought on by the job. What is the alternative? Let it fester? If that's the case, don't ask why you are being pulled from the street for excessive force. You might say to yourself: "I have not changed a damn thing on how I work," or "If my idiot boss cannot see that, then screw him," or "What the hell does he know anyway? He has not done shit in his career; not like I have!"

Well, ask yourself this. Did Joe Shit, the "rag man," really need those extra elbow strikes to the head? Hey! If he did, then by all means, show him some added "love," *but* it is time for real honesty here. I guarantee we have all been at the end of our rope. That's when you might be thinking something like, *You ran from me, punk, and now here is an elbow strike to the head because my kid mouthed off or because my wife smacked into another car or my daughter's boyfriend eyeballed her funny. I WILL BEAT THE LIVING SHIT OUT OF YOU, STUPID BASTARD!*

Life and this job catch up to you quick and it's not always easy to determine the difference. The question is: Are you justified? Perhaps, but think it through. While working street enforcement, I had a few basic rules erring on the side of caution. The following are two rules I created for myself, guidelines to keep me in check:

1. **Do not violate people's rights**. Ask yourself: Am I willing to sit in court and explain my actions, knowing full-well they were questionable? If the answer is anything but hell no, or hesitation happens here, it's time to go.

2. **Do not hurt people unnecessarily**. There is a time and place for "big fish" stories. In this case, they are not meant to cover up your actions. If the bad guy gets hurt, take them to the hospital. If someone runs or fights and does not end up getting transported, hospital is preferred, but for sure jail.

Generally, that meant *I* did something wrong. Assuming there were no handcuffs on and active aggression was in play. These are simple rules to abide by. They kept me straight. They were not hard to remember and were easy to justify to my boss, as well as in court. Do not forget.

We are the professionals!

CHAPTER THIRTY-FOUR
The Aftermath

People who take the leap into the life of a first responder are *unique*. I believe it is a calling that few partake in and even fewer still will ever fully understand, including those facing the daily horrors. Within the first responder community there **has** to be some sort of an understanding of the "unknown." In this chapter, we are looking at triggers, "emotional flashes" that occur when a memory of a critical incident is set off by a similar event. I say, "Work through them, but try not to over-analyze these 'flashes.' Just know that they are more common than you think and recognizing them is the better part of the battle."

Oftentimes, where the confusion starts is the lack of awareness. A lot of folks who have experienced these things might not reveal that the "flashes" occur for reasons of confusion, embarrassment, and denial—all potential factors here. Look, I'm no clinical expert on the subject, but I *can* tell you from experience … it is normal. I am going to go into detail about the triggers I have experienced and why they were significant to my growth.

TRIGGERS

#6807

Two weeks after my first *real* Officer-involved shooting I was cleared by the shrink and allowed to go back to the street. I eased back into patrol. While responding to a garden variety suspicious vehicle call, my back-up unit was on another call. It was a pretty busy day.

No biggie.

Of course, me, having just survived this major incident, I felt I had been promoted, if not thrust into the "big leagues" and could handle anything. Right?

Ha!

Foolishly, I went solo to the call. I found the "suspicious" car. My sergeant was heads up and decided to assist me, not just as a backup unit, but to see me in action and to gauge how I was performing. I approached the car just about the same time she arrived on scene. As if no time had passed, it hit me—a trigger, a full-blown flashback of my shooting. I stepped back before getting into the "kill zone," if you will, and looked for my boss. The fact that she was my boss had no bearing as to why I looked to her. What I later discovered was that I needed two things at that point:

1. A friendly face

2. Someone there to help keep me safe

193

I cannot explain why it occurred in that order, but it was what I needed at the time. The "suspicious" car turned out to be nothing worth investigating, but I walked away feeling like a hurdle had been overcome and that I was going to be alright. And I was. It was a good trigger.

A different type of trigger occurred later in 2011. Two good buddies of mine got into the wickedest gun fight and it all happened within view of the precinct. It was absolutely crazy! They both survived physically and, later on, mentally, which I have to say fills my heart with pride. My trigger occurred at the hospital later that day, not on the scene where you might expect, which is a topic for later.

I was in the hospital emergency room, along with dozens of hospital staff, Officers, brass, and blue family. There was a lot of joking, smiling, and laughing going on. Suddenly and from out of nowhere, I got physically shaky. It had been years, but the last time I was in a hospital setting under similar circumstances was when my great friend David Uribe, an outstanding Police Officer, gave his life for his community and friends in 2005 in an ambush. I had visited him at the hospital that day. I was told to prepare myself before entering his room because of how he looked. I broke down crying, refusing to remember him that way.

Six years later, I was flashing back. However, my thoughts in that event were *very* happy. We had two Officers who actually survived a

194

horrific gun battle, and we were all there together, able to speak with them, instead of having to see them for the last time. I was *never* happier to know that my friends were okay. It was pretty moving, and it was yet another good trigger.

After my final gunfight, I had two triggers back-to-back. The first occurred two months after the event. It was my first day back on the street. I was riding with my most trusted squad mate. Several hours into the shift, we responded to a call. A subject was making threats with a gun.

"Are you ready?" my squad mate asked.

"I guess we are going to find out."

It turned out the call was nothing more than a boy crying wolf, but the trigger came when I saw the first Officer on scene, one of my new buds from my last gunfight. Then another Officer from that scene showed up and then another until practically **everyone** from the last day I was on the street was there. I freaked.

"We gotta go," I said, turning to my partner. This guy is super intelligent and did not ask questions. He just hustled back to the car with me and let me vent. What I learned a few hours later, after my heart-rate settled, was that I had just returned to *the worst* scene of my life, in my mind. The trigger was seeing all those familiar faces. The difference being, despite the fact it was still an uncontrolled environment, I was safe. I was able to leave that scene safe. It was another good trigger.

Two days later, I was working an off-duty bar job. I was sitting on the tailgate of my truck when a guy in the bar next door drove off and fired ten rounds into the air. I jumped off the truck, ran straight to the road and tried to get a description of the car. It instantly dawned on me that I *still* had the ability to run to the sound of gunfire. Right then and there I knew I was going to be okay.

Good trigger.

It meant that I was on the right road to recovery. When I got sent *back* to the street, after having been sold a "bill of goods," (the brass promising a brand-new position that would keep me until my retirement), I had a hard time adjusting. For nearly seven months, I was sent to the rifle range as a rifle instructor. It was actually the perfect job for me, despite the fact that I was no longer chasing bad guys. I embraced the new position and a few weeks into it I started to really enjoy myself. However, I knew it was too good to be true. I held out as long as I could, but one day we were at the academy as a squad for the yearly training block. The instructors, different set of guys from the rifle squad, had set up multiple scenarios for us—normal training stuff. One particular set up was a traffic stop.

No biggie.

Wait! Yes. It was. It was an ambush scenario. Of course, they don't tell us that upfront, but by the end of the scenario I was shaking uncontrollably. It was the first time being shot at since the real thing.

Bad trigger.

The good thing was I recognized it almost immediately and I dealt with it. I opted out of the remainder of the training and went home feeling just fine. It was a bad scenario, but with a good ending ... not counting the anxiety attack.

More than a year and a half later, I was back on the street. Just another normal day, riding solo and feeling quite able-bodied and confident. An Officer-involved shooting comes over the radio and I am out on the hunt. Our bad guys had split up, one at the scene ... the other in the getaway car. And, yes, I just so *happened* to find the car. The trigger did not hit me until I received a couple of calls from a couple of different Dispatcher buddies, asking if I was okay.

"Christopher, we know you. You sounded *terrible* on the radio!"

What hit me was the fact that I had not responded to a serious life-threatening incident since my gunfight. I forgot *everything* I had learned about slowing time, tactical breathing and focusing on the task at hand. I made multiple mistakes and ended the day by having an "at-fault" collision. It was minor, as it turned out, but, nevertheless, it was my fault. My demons had not left me yet and although I *thought* I had processed through everything, the one thing that could have and ***did*** set me off was responding to another Officer-involved shooting.

Bad trigger.

How could I have prepared for that? A trigger like that can lay dormant for years before it *ever* surfaces. I write this, not to get you worked up about your own experience or to make you worry about what the future holds or to make you question what may or may not occur in the form of triggers for you. I want to reassure you that it is quite normal to experience this and share the thing that got me through each and every one of these episodes.

What got me through was simply acknowledging that they occurred. I took the time to dissect and analyze each one to figure out *why* the good were good and the bad were bad. One critical mistake I *did* make was when I was home for seven weeks after the gunfight. In that time, I created my own triggers in my head, telling myself, if not predicting what my triggers would look like. And, of course, when those *real* triggers hit, they were circumstances I never even considered. My point is, do *not* try and anticipate your triggers as you go. You will likely be wrong. Don't create more work for yourself. I have been on both sides of the emotional fence, and I have made mistakes that took unnecessary time away from my healthy recovery. Let the triggers occur naturally. Let it be a healthy fight.

CHAPTER THIRTY-FIVE
Street Smarts

It was a routine traffic stop with a truckload of dudes, your garden variety of guys who were out of place and just dangerous-looking enough for me to prep my gun. They were begging to be stopped and I was only happy to oblige. I got all four occupants out of the truck and onto the sidewalk. There were several Officers hanging around, as I was searching the driver side of the vehicle. The driver, himself, was also on the sidewalk with a clear view of me rifling through his things. At the time, I was wearing my outer carrier with my Glock .45 snapped into the vest—normal everyday carry. It was business as usual, until "Murphy" thought it would be hilarious for my .45 to pop out of my vest and drop onto the ground while I was bent over, checking under the front seat.

Dumbass.

Embarrassed, I looked up and made eye contact with the driver. Yeah. He saw it happen.

Damn it!

He was probably thinking, *I am in handcuffs, and you can't even secure your own weapon.* And he would have been right. By some small miracle, my fellow loudmouths (i.e., Officers) did not see my epic fail. So, I was hoping that it would be our little secret, mine, and the driver's. I didn't find anything in the truck. I did, however, find traffic charges that could have landed this guy in jail, and he knew it. As I approached him, my demeanor became dead serious.

"So, you know I got you for some traffic charges. Right?"

"Yup."

"Okay," I said, visually scanning left and then right. "I am going to make you a deal. If you swear never to tell anyone that you saw me drop my gun, you are free to go."

The guy busted out laughing and responded, "Absolutely, sir!"

I turned and walked away with both my tail and my gun tucked. Thank God for the indestructible, Cop-proof, Glock .45. That was a real lesson in humility.

Typically, it was easy finding criminals. I mean, they weren't exactly subtle in their getaway. When bad guys see a Cop, they usually slam on the brakes, make a hard turn, and then reappear at the next intersection. Oh, and they give you "the look," a culpable expression not lost on me.

Gotcha!

There is *definitely* a science to catching criminals, on top of which, bad guys are characteristically not that bright. Throw in the fear of escaping the "heat," and the lack of proficiency in forward-thinking, not to mention the chemical alterations caused by drug use, it simply meant a few minor adjustments on my part to perfect the art of sneaking and peeking. I used to joke that I could tell whether someone had a suspended license, a felony warrant or just beat their kid from "the look" they gave. I got that part of it down pat and would always let the suspicious person make the first move before I decided whether or not to make contact. It turned out that I was pretty lucky *most* of the time.

One of the greatest lessons I learned in chasing bad guys was from a K9 handler who would later become an icon for me. We were chasing a dude through a neighborhood.

No biggie.

He jumped into a fenced yard. Our first backup unit was the K9 handler.

"Whatcha guys got?" he asked.

"Stolen car. Dude ran and reached in his waistband."

"Where did you see him last."

"Here in this yard," I said, catching my breath.

"Did you lock down the next street?"

"Not yet we decided to wait and listen."

The K9 handler looked like a proud father watching his boy chuck the football down to the end zone for a touchdown. A little while later, we caught knucklehead and the K9 handler said something that forever changed how I did my thing. He said, "I can't believe you guys had the foresight to sit, wait and listen. That's absolutely priceless!"

I hadn't really thought about it, but okay! Looking back, it made perfect sense. After learning more about the K9 handler, and appreciating the merit behind his praise, considering his talent, stature, and reputation with the department, I started thinking more definitively into the tactic of "waiting and listening." That said, we did get a little ass-chewing for standing in the wide-open street versus behind concealment, but a good lesson was learned just the same. It was a good fight, not to mention a good reason for me to remain on the street as a patrol Officer.

There was a time, early on in my career, when I considered moving up to detective. However, when I learned that detectives are mostly involved with follow up stuff on the computer and telephone, having very little street contact, it lost its appeal for a rook wanting to save the world. At least as a street Cop I would get to carry a gun, jump fences and drive fast cars in pursuit of the law. That was always the dream!

CHAPTER THIRTY-SIX
The Culmination

I don't know how or exactly when it happened, but at some point, I reached my emotional limit. It was February 2016, and I was working patrol, the part of my detail that, from time to time, I really did *not* enjoy. I was back on the street, responding to another emergency call—trouble unknown. Fire was responding.

No biggie!

I was a veteran, in nearly every sense of the word, so I just took it as another "call." That was until I arrived on the scene. I was less than half a mile away. I rolled up with Fire and was the first first-responder in the house. That's when I heard the screaming. It seemed like loud cries were coming from every room in the house.

What is going on?

I was directed to a bedroom in the back. There, I found a large man in his thirties on his knees doing everything he could to save his nephew's life. The boy was eight years old. It was his sister's twelfth birthday party when he decided to tie one end of a shoelace around his neck and the other end around a clothing rod in his closet. He took one small step off of a piece of furniture that he had purposely placed beneath him. I wasn't sure if it was intentional or if it was a botched attempt at the trending "asphyxiation high" game. I never got the gist of that game, but it made me wonder. What fucking eight-year-old would *ever* think of this on his own? And, if it wasn't intentional, did he even understand the risks or consequences of his actions? There is a lot about this world I do not understand and, in that moment, I felt as helpless as I ever have. All I could do was console the uncle who was the only one *brave* enough to make an attempt at saving this kid's life.

Meanwhile, Fire went to work. I had a small hand in helping to load the boy's lifeless body onto the stretcher. He was already cold to the touch. I knew enough to know *exactly* what that meant.

No way is this kid coming back.

Without any direction or warning or anything of the kind, I hopped into the back of the ambulance with the boy and made the long journey to the children's hospital. I'm still not sure what prompted me to do so, but I did, nonetheless. Once I was there, I wandered aimlessly through the halls, took two phone calls from the brass, a lieutenant, and a commander, neither of whom I worked for and reported all that I knew. I took two more incoming phone calls from Dispatcher buddies of mine.

Okay. Breathe!

"Are you ok?"

"Of course! Why" I asked.

"I heard what happened and just wanted to make sure. You sounded pretty bad on the radio."

Ok. I suppose there is no point in arguing.

"Hey man! You left your car at the scene."

Damn it! So, I did.

It hit me that I had no way back to my area. I made a few phone calls in an attempt to retrieve my car. It turned out that was totally unnecessary because my friends had already made arrangements for me.

Thanks, guys!

I mentioned earlier that I drove back to a precinct I no longer worked at. Well, *that* was the day. This was a clue that I was quickly nearing my limit.

The next major incident happened a month or so later, a shooting call which led to a supervisor putting me in a serious, potentially deadly-force situation. It was a valid shooting with the suspect identified as female, and the shooting victim, a "true victim," a good, solid citizen, was alive and in need of medical attention. I was exposed, downrange of no less than five rifles, multiple calibers, not to mention a lunatic whose male roommate had calculations for ammonium nitrate, a manifesto written out, the *Anarchist's Cookbook*, multiple weapons and at least 1,500 rounds of ammunition at the ready.

Not good.

This was a failure on so many levels. When I started screaming out the "red flags" to the Feds, I had concrete reason to believe this guy, the roommate, was a serious threat. However, nothing was ever followed up on, despite the initial "interest." The shooting suspect's roommate, a serious bad guy, started making threats against us after the initial shooting call, and yet was let go pending no charges. On top of which, two close buddies of mine got into a wicked gunfight later that same night, unrelated incident, both survived.

Thank the Lord.

It always bothered me that I was not available to help them. A few weeks passed and my role in the original shooting investigation was complete. One day while I was home, I got a call from a squad mate, asking if I had seen the news. I hadn't.

I hate those calls.

As it happened, the bad guy who was let go "pending no charges," was released simply because those on scene wanted to secure and go home for the day. Because they did not book this criminal, he was free to drive out of town and do a drug rip. He ended up killing three people before heading back to town and, if that weren't enough, he decided to take a shot at a patrol supervisor from another agency. The round went through his windshield and into his headrest, missed him by fractions of an inch, but only because the sergeant was getting out of his patrol car at the time it happened. My anxiety was building momentum at an alarming rate, and I was headed straight for a brick wall. Six weeks later, we lost David Glasser. It took me more than two years to come to the realization that my career ended the day David was killed. On many counts, I retired that day. I just didn't know it. When I tell the story of the eight-year-old boy who hanged himself in the closet, it is always very vague—purposely not a lot of detail. As I run my hand across the bridge of my nose, I can say in sincere honesty, "I was already up to here, emotionally-speaking." My failure was not recognizing it as it was occurring. This was a huge mistake! There were plenty of clues, but I still failed to recognize them. I was probably too stupid and too arrogant to believe that this was anything more than just "my job." Had I taken the necessary steps to remove myself from my chosen profession from time to time, to decompress, I *might* have been able to stick it out a little longer before losing it. Maybe not, but knowing what I know now, it seems obvious to me. And when the really "big one" came, the day David was killed, I was too far behind the curve to recover in a timelier manner. For the record, however, I *did* recover, fully and proudly. It wasn't easy. Writing this book helped. It also lets folks know that things like this do happen, and the chance of getting "fixed" is quite good, so long as you recognize it, accept it, and move forward.

CHAPTER THIRTY-SEVEN
The Day it Happened

Three rounds were fired. David was hit twice, unbeknownst to me at the time. He went down. Gunfire erupted. All hell broke loose, and my life would never be the same. Moments prior, I had shifted from the driver's seat to the rear of my car and then into the street. Shots fired, I was poised and ready, covering the front door and window of the house—still kind of fat, dumb and happy. I'd been here before—no biggie. My reaction time to fire back was no more than two-and-half seconds. I did what I was trained to do:

1. Find a target

2. Get a sight picture

3. Safety catch off

4. Finger on the trigger

5. Fire

It was another shooting. I'd been here before, but it felt like a bigger deal. One week later, during the investigation, I was asked, "What was your sight picture/target and what was your background?"

I did not have a solid answer, but my thought process was this: I could see there was no threat from the house. That was *my* area of responsibility. I heard gunfire, a lot of gunfire and it was coming from inside the van. I had a weapon system that could do a couple of things in this situation:

1. Stop the threat immediately

2. Suppress fire, give this guy some pause

Knowing what I know now, I really wish it had been the first versus the latter. I picked a spot in the center of the passenger side window and fired a volley from "Delilah," my trusty Colt AR-15.

That should do it. Yeah?

No. "Murphy," that asshole that ruins shit for Cops, arrived on scene. It was an over the shoulder, blind shot through the skinny crack of a car door, a one in a million round that bad guys take that struck and killed Dave. Meanwhile, ass-head, our suicidal suspect, continued to evade a barrage of gunfire from six responding Officers, including a second rifle operator from about ten yards away. That's when he pointed his weapon in my direction and returned fire at me. The entire gunfight was approximately four seconds of utter chaos. Not that it mattered much, but I did what I had to do. I guarantee that if I was put back into that situation again, I would do it the same. The investigators were good with my decision to fire. And then another question followed.

"Hey, you guys were getting shot at ... right?"

"Sir ... yes, sir!"

"Who else was inside the van?"

"Well, I was there 13 minutes, and no one came or went from inside the van."

Was I to believe whoever was inside the van did not have a plan? I'm thinking if you were in the van and you knew what was about to occur and you did nothing to stop it, then you are *not* a victim. Unless you were a hostage, in which case, I would have seen some activity and the entire dynamic would have changed. Luckily there wasn't anyone else involved.

There was a total of six rounds fired from the van. Not that I was counting, but I personally heard *and* felt three of them buzz by me?

Yeah.

And the first three rounds were David's. I wouldn't realize it until later in the day, but David went down and he, alone, was the angel on my shoulder, keeping me safe.

Thank you, my brother!

When I realized *I* was being fired at, I had three thoughts:

1.   Wait! I do not like this anymore.

2.   I want to run away.

3. Oh, you mother fucker! You just shot at me. You want to

play? I can play!

I felt rage, anger like I had never felt before.

What do I do here?

My options were limited. That's when I let loose another volley--

15 or more rounds. There will be no running away. Stand and deliver. One

and done ... right?

Yeah.

We tried that. It didn't work. We were getting shot at and the

biggest gun I was allowed to carry, my Delilah, wasn't working.

Now what?

Fortunately, I paid attention in class. Forget the fact I was a

certified firearms and rifle instructor, so I quickly started thinking. There

was no time to call for support.

What if I change my angle? That might work.

My first volley was at a 30-degree angle. I thought if I could

square up more, I could put him down. I did a Matrix-like jump from one

side of the street to the other, in about one and a half steps, and returned for

a second volley. In haste, I started shooting before I was on target, putting

the first five rounds in the middle part of his passenger door. It wasn't bad,

as it turned out. My hits were solid, but I wanted better. So, I got my sight picture and hit him where it counted ... again and again. During my first volley, I was looking through the non-magnified optic red-dot style—zero front sight. During my second volley, the entire optic was one giant red dot. I suspect, at that point, I was literally seeing red.

After my second volley, one and a half seconds totaling 15 rounds, by my estimation, I felt it was safe to approach the van. If our bad guy survived *that* volley, I did not want to think about what I would have to do next. That's when things went a little screwy in my head. Mind you:

> - I had fired 22 rounds—total
> - There were two separate volleys of fire
> - Officers were screaming into my earpiece, yet I heard nothing, but the faint clink of brass hitting the pavement and glass shattering in the driveway
> - I did *not* hear Delilah, a 151-decibel rifle, fire.

Strange phenomenon!

After that, things *really* got strange. Part of the reason I did not hear anything was because the radios locked up for two solid minutes. Seems the entire city switched over to the channel we were on, basically crashing the entire system. No Officers could clear out and the Dispatcher was unable to type any messages or even clear on her radio. I later learned about the protocol for Dispatchers during these types of critical incidents and what they go through, as well. Our Dispatcher did everything perfectly and, like me, blamed herself for failing. It took one year, but I, personally put that self-sabotaging thought to rest, not only for me, but for her as well.

As I made my way over to the Tahoe blocking the van, David's Tahoe, I saw another Officer standing to my right ... just behind me. I tried to get a bead on the bad guy, but I could not see what I needed. Approaching the van was an option, but it didn't seem very sound at the time. At that point, I did something I never do, not even on the range, despite knowing full-well that it is a life-saving tactic. I checked my world. I looked around to see what other threats were present. That is when I saw the Officer standing in the street, a really good guy, a field training officer, a rifle operator, and an overall good Cop. He was standing in the middle of the street in combat lock, rifle slung, ghost-white, staring into space. Suddenly I was confused.

Why is he standing there in shock?

I screamed at him to cover the door and he quickly snapped to attention and covered down on his sector of fire. Later we discussed the event and I apologized for my harsh words.

"That's what I needed to get back into the fight," he said.

From there, I moved to the driver's side of the Tahoe. I did not like my view of shithead. I asked another Officer to take my spot on the passenger side of the Tahoe. When I got to the rear, I ran into the sergeant in charge of the scene, a man who is now a very good friend of mine. He was standing behind the patrol car holding his radio, looking extremely pissed. I knew he was an angry type of guy, but the expression on his face was something completely different. It was not normal, and confusion set in once again. I had a plan, so I kept moving. Just about the same time the sergeant in charge began purposefully walking in the same direction as me. We later joked about it. I teased that he took *my* spot, but that was not what he had in mind. His plan was much simpler than mine. He was going to walk past the Tahoe, up the driveway to the driver's side of the van and execute this monster. Knowing this now, I, personally, have *no* problem with that, but wait a second. This fight was not over. As the sergeant stormed past the Tahoe, it dawned on me that he was not stopping. He was going all the way in.

Umm ... excuse me, boss! I think that is a bad idea.

That's when I jumped in, grabbing him from behind and getting into a serious scrape. It was your basic knock-down, drag-out struggle in the driveway between a plain clothes Cop and a sergeant. Now, this particular sergeant could surely have cleaned my clock anytime he wanted, but he admitted later that he had no memory, whatsoever, of that happening. This was good for me, since I was on full-blown autopilot and not thinking straight. I was, however, able to overpower him and send him back to the rear of the Tahoe. He was out of control. What the hell was he thinking? No time to process that ... back to work. I attempted to get another sight picture on our bad guy from the driver's side of the Tahoe.

Damn it! I still can't see enough of him.

Another Officer, the fourth one I had seen at that point, approached me from behind for support. "David's hit," he yelled.

Officer down?

The reality of what was unfolding began to sink in. I was consumed with both fear and anxiety.

(Unconscious combat breath).

It wouldn't be until later that I would learn what ***that*** breath was.

Thanks, Lt. Colonel Grossman!

Magazine exchange and I was back in the fight. They were working on David across the street.

Fuck! This is bad.

Focus and breathe.

"Put a Tahoe in that driveway!" I shouted, pointing to the left of the van. It sounded more like a demand than a request.

Sorry about that, my brother.

Two minutes later, the Tahoe was moved into position. In that time, I cleared for help, assistance that would not arrive. I was angry, but later realized *why* that help did not show, and that was just fine. I covered my spot and moved into position at the Tahoe in the driveway to the north. It had been 12 long minutes. It was hot outside—no less than 103 degrees. The hood of the Tahoe was burning hot. I was in short sleeves with a clear view of shithead. I was just ten yards away. I clicked down a bead on my optic, asking him to move.

Take a breath. Move a finger ... anything and I will drill your temple.

As a Christian man, I knew I could not take that shot, but as an angry, revenge-seeking man I desperately wrestled with wanting to. I decided, then and there, having to answer to my brass or, worse yet, my own God, was not something I was willing to do. This is still a struggle for me, all these years later.

Over the next 12 minutes, my view of bad guy shrank. I'm pretty sure I held my breath for the majority of that time, and I am positive I never blinked. By the time I was physically relieved of my duty, I was looking through a straw hole. It was tunnel vision, straight up combat-lock. I was so focused; I could not focus.

My relief came in the form of a SWAT operator. He called my name several times. He got no response. This hulk of a man could see I was lights out. He knew that I needed a little nudge. Mind you, a little nudge for him was like a professional hockey player checking his competitor into the glass, as far as I was concerned. Crazy SWAT guys! He was right to check me. That "nudge" got me *back* into the fight, which fortunately for me was over. I will never forget his words.

"We got you, man. Walk this way."

I was bunkered out of the scene and into the street. I was safe, but what was next? I went into auto-pilot.

Where do you go from there?

Give me a job ... something to do. It was too late for that. The boss was there. I said something to him and then wrapped my arm around his neck. He had a look of utter despair on his face. That's when the adrenaline began to wear off and I physically began to unravel. I walked to the end of the street. There was a lot of activity—fire personnel, Officers everywhere. It was chaos. I will find him someday, but a young Officer who I did not recognize was standing in the road.

"Gimme your phone," I demanded, as if he was one of my own children. He could see I was not okay, so he handed me his cell phone, at which time, my hands were shaking so badly I could not even dial. I handed the phone back to him and asked him to dial my home number.

When I heard her voice, I crumbled. It suddenly occurred to me what had just taken place, the worst thing that would ever happen in my career. I broke down and cried, as I told my wife the news. After a brief and somewhat fumbled conversation, I went to hand the Officer his phone. It was drenched in tears and snot, so I made a feeble attempt at wiping it clean.

"I got it," he said. By then, he, too, was sobbing. The surrounding first responders, no less than a dozen men, were all in tears.

Oops! Sorry, guys! That was not my plan.

CHAPTER THIRTY-EIGHT
Lessons from David's Day

There are so many lessons I took away from that fateful day, David's day. I am a Christian man. I believe in a higher power, but I do not attend church regularly for my own personal reasons. However, I do find my peace with God on a regular basis in *my* church, in those "God spots" found deep in the woods beneath a tree, next to a creek hidden on the side of a mountain or seaside at sunset.

LESSON ONE: SELF-SACRIFICE

Dave was spiritual. He loved the Lord. What I did *not* know, however, was just **how much he loved Him**. He loved Him so much that he willingly gave up his life to meet his God. I still can't comprehend that, but I fully admit that I am learning. Personally, I am of the belief that Dave stood beside me, protecting me during my portion of the gunfight after he fell. And, of course, not just alongside me, but *all* the folks who were in harm's way that day.

I remember one day, not long after Dave's day, I was carpooling with a close friend of mine from the academy, a former boss who is a specialist in his own right. He is someone who regularly keeps me in check. He was driving that day. We weren't discussing the shooting or anything terribly important when he asked, "Hey, do you think after Dave realized he was gone, he stood up and said, 'Okay. I'm ready. Take me?'"

A warm feeling washed over me and, well, then it all hit me like a sledgehammer to the temple ... again!

Gotta quit that shit!

I have had this conversation with folks before, people I love dearly, believers who would respond to that same question with, "No. It was the hand of God that decided, not David."

Here is my argument, what *I* believe to be true. I am fully convinced David saw the danger upon us all and told God, "No! I am it. Take just me."

Of course, the God-fearing folk might believe only God, Himself, can determine your day. I disagree in this particular case. I believe with all my heart that David sacrificed his life for his beliefs, but I also believe without a doubt that he also sacrificed his life for his buddies and me. He is what kept us alive. Yes. I know that theory, in and of itself, can be a struggle, but I think David's sacrifice reads like psalm John 15:13 in the Bible, "Greater love hath no man than this ... that a man lay down his life for his friends." Self-sacrifice. Who could argue that? No one I know.

This lesson, in my humble opinion, is about being right with YOUR God. If you're willing to die for your beliefs, as David was, I believe you can conquer anything, never fearing death when your time comes. If, like David, you can do that ... your legacy will forever remain in the hearts, minds, and souls of those whose lives you have touched, if not saved.

LESSON TWO: ACTION VS. REACTION

On the tactical side of things, I knew about and had practiced, though never actually put into deployment the theory of action versus reaction. I'd say it is a pretty important theory and necessary to understand. I don't know the science behind it, but there is a company who puts on a fantastic class explaining the dynamics of it. For me "action vs. reaction" was simple. I used a training drill from the rifle range. Of course, virtually any range will work and is not limited to rifles. There is a name for this drill, but for the purpose of liability, I will explain what the drill looks like:

- ✓ All standing. All static.
- ✓ 20 yards: 10 rounds, 10 seconds.
- ✓ 10 yards: 10 rounds, five seconds.
- ✓ Five yards: 10 rounds, two and a half seconds.
- ✓ All rounds must hit within an eight-inch circle.

It is a "stand and deliver" drill and I believe it was the two and a half second portion of the training that may have saved my life. I have seen guys shoot ten rounds under two seconds—semi-automatic.

That's moving!

Obviously, it can and should be altered or customized, depending upon circumstance. Imagination is the key here. Think of real gunfight scenarios and adapt. I lecture to my students all the time that if I can put ten rifle rounds in you in two and a half seconds, the probability of you surviving is unlikely. All conditions considered, you must account for two and a half seconds to get a sight picture and fire, taking into account bone support, breathing, muscle relaxation, etc.

What can be done in two and a half seconds? You can take or you can deliver ten rounds. That's what! Ten rounds is a relatively low number, if you think about it, but like I said, those ten rounds can do a significant amount of damage. And your reaction time can add or subtract rounds, especially if your opponent is dedicated or, God forbid, he is well-trained.

Imagine, if you will, you take a good, strong stance, aim in nicely, take that combat breath and squeeze off a shot.

Oh ... wait!

This is not a simulator, and it is not shooting paper in a sterile environment with safety instructors and peers wanting to move to the next drill before lunch. **This is gun-fighting, no points for second place**. Listen, nobody trains harder than Cops, but if a Cop can pull this drill off, than you know a bad guy can, too. Remember Murphy?

Yeah.

Murphy always errs on the side of the bad guy. Lesson learned and enough said. Ask yourself this question: How long will it take your brain to process what has happened in that gunfight scenario? How long will it take for you to decide to act, take all the necessary steps to act, and then engage? These are things to consider on a case-by-case basis. That being said, train hard, my friends!

LESSON THREE: FAILURE

Failure is a good teacher, but let's face it … failure in a gunfight could mean serious injury and/or death, unless you're like me and you have your own personal David Glasser to save your skin. And, if that's the case, good on you! You're one of the lucky ones. So, how do we succeed in gun fights? I say we train! **We train like we mean it, seriously and hardcore**. There is plenty of time offline to joke around and bust chops. However, when we are online, let's get it on!

First things first: **Know your equipment thoroughly**, beyond what you have in your mag pouch and where your flashlight is mounted. That's not what I'm talking about here.

No.

Prone yourself out in your kit or uniform. Practice

getting your secondary weapon out of its hiding place and know with full

certainty what the capabilities are of the weapon system you are carrying.

Believe me when I say, you will want to figure this out on the range in

your own time, *not* on the street in real time!

Master the basics. **Repetition is a must** and, when you feel

confident, move on to skill sets that are only limited to your imagination.

It's true; there are range limitations, but be creative. One silly drill I used

to practice was using a laser light, your average cat toy.

Cop salary. Remember?

I mounted the laser light (i.e., cat toy) to my barrel and taped a

paper plate to the target. I was limited by distance, but I was not limited to

constant on flood lights. So, in total darkness, I kept the laser pointed at the

paper plate and I would walk and walk and walk and walk. I kept this up

until I had honed my skills well enough that I could walk from the end of

the range to the front, all while keeping the bright, red dot dead on the

plate. When I mastered that skill, I advanced by adding the task of

shooting, making sure so as not to stop between shots, but rather to keep

moving forward in a fluid motion. You can see how simple this exercise is and yet how it can improve one's strengths and abilities on a much larger scale. Say, if you ever find yourself in a gunfight.

A buddy of mine tapes a party balloon to his kid's radio-controlled car to create a moving target—ingenious! How often do we ever train on moving targets? I'll let you in on a little secret. Bad guys don't sit still and let you shoot them. They *will* be moving, shooting, and hiding. And who knows what else?

For me, during my gunfight, there were two failures:

1. During my first volley, my rounds did not connect. The bad guy was still alive—failure.

2. My second volley, I fired five rounds into the metal portion of the door. The good thing about this tactic, if you want to call it that, is that, oftentimes, those hollow points we like to carry will turn into ball rounds and do some damage. So, you'd better know your target and its surroundings. This is true for aluminum garage doors, as well. Be aware. I've seen it happen. Four of those five rounds made their way through the van door, and they found their mark. Number five, however, did *not*. Something in the mechanical portion of the door stopped it before it went through—failure.

Are those two outcomes truly failures? Not necessarily,

considering the dynamics of this particular gunfight. However, that is *exactly* my point. I think we can agree that a gunfight is a "dynamic" situation and that I was behind the curve. Honestly, it was only by divine intervention that I was spared. With that said, **do not allow yourself to be behind the curve**. By the very nature of our business, you will find yourself behind the curve at times, but there are ways to overcome, if you take this job seriously. Play when you can, but above all things, take it seriously. Remember, just 30 minutes before the gunfight of my life, I was sitting at a computer impounding weed.

LESSON FOUR: SAY WHAT YOU NEED TO SAY

I am not superstitious, but it has been my experience that when folks tell me to "be careful" while on the job, it has always brought me bad luck … like near-death, close call kind of bad luck. Is it all just mental, a self-fulfilling prophecy thing? Perhaps it is.

Some might say *I* am mental, but this phenomenon is surely based on fact. It started long before my days as a Cop, but when it crept into my professional world, believe me, I paid close attention. Let me explain. Following the gunfight, I spent some time at the hospital where they transported Dave. From there was the long drive back to the station and then home, finally. It was three o'clock in the morning—21 hours from the time I started my shift.

When I got home, I collapsed into bed. I slept an hour, one single hour. I woke up the next day and got on the phone—sort of. It took me about two hours of scanning through text messages and voicemails before I could actually start the return phone calls. I had received 78 text messages and 25 voicemails—no duplicates. Trust me when I say, there are more people in the world than you think who actually give a damn.

I got through every message. The last message I read was the first in the stack, the very first message I received. It was from a close friend of mine. I had seen her as I was walking out the door to respond to the call. Her text message came in right about the time I got eyes on the house. (It read: "Be careful. ♥♥") She couldn't have known that those two words were somewhat of an omen for me and because she was (and still is) a close friend, I had to let her know what I was feeling. I tried as hard as I could to be delicate, but I knew what was coming.

"Hey, that message you sent ..." I said. "You were the last person to communicate with me before the shooting started?"

She offered a tearful apology, which I absolutely dismissed.

"Oh my god," she cried. "I'd have been the last to talk to you."

More tears.

"Okay. Stop. I am fine. See."

It was a hard conversation to have, but I felt it had to be.

Say what you need to say ... right?

That was something Dave was brilliant at. He would always leave his family and friends with the words "I love you." It was a simple, yet profound gesture. As first responders, the dangers are great and ever-present. Anything can happen at any given time, so you'd best make sure your loved ones are aware that you do, indeed and undoubtedly, love them because that opportunity could be stolen.

That day I did my best to convince more than one of my friends that I was alright. My exact words were, "Look! I'm standing right here in front of you. See." It's overwhelming and, oftentimes, in these stressful circumstances, the hardest part for people to realize is that you survived, that you are not dead, even if you are standing right in front of them.

LESSON FIVE: SPIRITUALITY VS. RELIGION

Spirituality is not my strong suit. I do, however, take spiritual lesson with these things as they come. At least that is what I would have believed before May 18, 2016. As I mentioned, I do not regularly attend church. However, I am drawn to the rich spirituality of the universe. In my opinion, spirituality and religion are ***not*** the same.

Someone very close to me taught me that spirituality is a feeling, a sense of beauty and an appreciation for what God has given us. The question I am regularly asked is, *"Where does beauty come from?"*

Well, look at the mountains. Look at the ocean and at the setting sun, as it turns into brilliant colors. Where does that come from? The answer to that question can stir a lot of debate, but I discovered that the whole point of the question is not what I think or what you or anyone else thinks. The answer to the question is simply this: Stop and look. Look around you and take it all in from time to time.

I know for a fact that no one reading these words will argue that there is more ugliness in the world than we need, but how often do we actually take time to appreciate what is beautiful? I mean, how often do you purposefully stop what you are doing and look for it. How often do you take time to appreciate the beautiful things? That, for me, is spirituality. As for religion, I will reserve my opinion for one-on-one discussions.

Another friend of mine, a true warrior and as humble as they come, shared with me his story and struggle. His was a wicked, nasty gunfight, an ambush. Both he and his partner prevailed. Superior mindset and tactics won that gunfight. It's not my story to tell, but this man was scrutinized for praying over the bad guy who was killed during the confrontation. Weeks later, while relaxing on his porch, he suddenly burst into tears. When asked why he was crying, my friend could not explain, except to say that God had spoken to him. God's words were, "Now you understand the struggle I felt having to decide who to bring home."

That story gives me chills. How can you argue it? Why would you want to? It is only for my friend's soul to understand and, possibly to absolve. Like me, he was spared for a reason only God knows.

So, what does all this mean? I don't know, but I do know that after carpooling to work with my friend, as mentioned in Lesson One, following the heavy conversation of whether or not Dave honorably stood up to God that day, so that his fellow Officers, guys like me, could live to fight another day, something astonishing happened. I went to my shrink, and I told her all about that conversation. The reaction I got was completely unexpected. She started bawling and the realization of what was happening started to unfold.

We chatted about it several more times, but on the day I told her, I hopped on my bike and rode straight to the cemetery. I remember feeling pretty good, almost refreshed when I got there. I don't know why, but I had the stupidest, shit-eating grin on my face. I knelt next to Dave's headstone and said a small prayer. I read the words in stone written by his babies and the quotes carved into the slab. Then I turned toward the sky and with a full heart I said, "Thanks, man! I love you."

It felt good. I have no idea what purpose it served, but I kind of figured it didn't make much difference. I know Dave heard me and that's all that mattered. As soon as I got home, I called his mom. I told her all about it.

"I love that you told me," she replied. "And please keep doing so. The truth is I hear these stories all the time about Davey."

Man! What an amazing human being he was and, for so many of us, will always be.

CHAPTER THIRTY-NINE
Back to the Scene

Warning: This is a touchy subject, so let me start by saying that I have seen and can appreciate both sides of the spectrum here: Firstly, the need to look in the rearview and remember a critical incident and secondly, the need to bury it—deep. The problem with burying bad memories is that unless you retire from the department or move to a whole new part of town, the chances of you unintentionally ending up back "on the scene" is highly likely, especially if you live in a small community. Personally, I believe facing these issues head on is the best approach, but I also realize that everyone is different, and no one can make you face anything you are not ready or willing to deal with.

On this particular topic, it comes down to awareness, recognizing potential issues that should be raised to the surface before an Officer has no choice but to go *back* to the scene. Imagine if you will … the radio call comes out. You are dispatched to a scene, an area of town where there are still some "demons" lurking in your past, and the realization sets in, along with the anxiety of facing the unknown upon arrival. If you, as an Officer, have not faced those "demons" and you have to return to a place, where the worst day of your professional life has occurred, it can go badly, if not turn deadly. Those bad triggers I mentioned may hit you during the call. And that is *not* the time or the place to be dealing with them. These issues can be worked through, but it takes the "village," if you will, to get it done.

Having a good support system in place is the key.

Having a boss and/or squad mates in your corner, people who can recognize the potential for disaster, is what I am talking about. Without anticipating and planning for such an event, how can anyone prepare for it? And remember, you are answering a call, dealing with citizens who do not understand or, in some cases, care that you are having an "episode" and just want their issue solved. Which I am sorry to say is their right, mostly.

When I went back to Dave's scene, I was numb—*completely* numb. I spent the entire day stopping off at different locations, trying to face it all. It was a good plan, but it was too much, too soon, a mere five days following the incident. I went to the precinct first, then the scene. After that I went to the range and then to headquarters. I spent an entire day reliving Dave's day. For me, visiting each place was healthy. However, perhaps it would have been best not to visit them all at once.

The precinct was rough because I was immediately met with

David's patrol car in the parking lot. It gave me pause. Apparently, it had been returned and no one knew what to do with it. I had driven that car for a few years before it became surplus to the JVs. I was very surprised to see it in the lot. I met with the secondary supervisor who was called to secure the scene. We spoke for at least an hour and, of course, recapped the event. I saw a handful of Officers, exchanged hugs with them and then finally headed back to the scene of the crime. It was a 30-minute-drive filled with all the anticipation.

Upon arrival, I parked in the same lot where I had spent my last moments alone before being sent away that dreadful day. I let it all sink in. I then took a nervous stroll down the sidewalk toward a patrol car where an Officer kept watch over the scene, a security guard, of sorts, turned collector. He had a bag of cash and checks on his dashboard. Everyday folks were stopping by and giving monetary donations, stuffed animals, and other gifts. Some local elementary school kids drew a huge badge in chalk on the sidewalk with a ton of handwritten messages next to it. I was so overwhelmed that I never even thought to take a picture of it. Instead, I proceeded to the spot where it all went down. As I got within view of the driveway, my heart started to race. Panic was setting in. I walked past, as if not even planning to stop, then I turned around to look from the view I originally had from my undercover car. This was totally unplanned.

I stood across the street, my feet planted in the ground in imaginary cement. I could not push forward. Not even realizing it, I stood in silence for several minutes. I approached the sacred ground and started to tear up. Staring at the pavement where I knew David had been robbed of his last breath, I was motionless, asking the question, *"Why?"*

I did not stay very long. I don't know why. Was it too much reality? Was I too scared? Was I feeling helpless, vulnerable, anxious and at an utter loss for reasoning? Who knows? It was my first time back. I was not sure what to think. So, I headed to the academy range. I needed to get qualified on the internal affairs weapon that was given to me. Because of some strange "supervisory denial," combined with a policy I was not aware of, I did *not* get to qual. However, I was told I could carry the weapon, even for off duty work.

Okay.

While at the range, I ran into some folks I knew and, again, recapped the horrible event. I was beginning to dislike the comment, "Glad to see you're okay."

We were standing on the dirt, watching a couple of folks loading magazines and chatting amongst themselves. They were Officers from a different agency, guys who had no idea who I was or why I was there. I thought nothing of it. I remember watching as they approached the line and made the safety announcement, "We're going hot!"

Alrighty!

One shot … just one shot and I jumped like a gymnast on the mat. That one shot caught me completely off guard. It threw me for a loop. I turned ghost-white. I remember my range buddy grabbing me by the shoulders and repeatedly asking me, "Are you okay?"

I guess not.

"I'm fine," I laughed, secretly unsure. That was the only time I was startled by gunfire after the event that changed my life, and it may very well have been the first time I started to question my sanity.

What is wrong with me?

No one is immune to a startled response, but I was watching these men load their magazines and I knew **exactly** what was coming. Combat stress/flashback? I suppose. I was beginning to have a vague understanding as to why military combat veterans commonly dive under tables after hearing exhaust pipes backfire and similar loud, abrupt noises. One (anticipated) shot and I was a mess. I often wonder if there had been a longer volley of gunfire, if I would have been okay. Who knows?

I truly cannot fathom what our military combat heroes are forced to endure. God bless them for facing those horrors and going back to do it again and again. I imagine they make it back to the makeshift base in country and have a major sigh of relief, but then within 12 hours or maybe a few days they are right back at it again. How do they muster that kind of courage?

Returning to the scene filled with bad memories and horrific details is *never* easy. I suggest bringing a trusty companion along. However, keep in mind, **this journey is about you and the road to healing**. Yes. I say be selfish. If you are standing at "the scene" and you are alive, I would say you have earned the right to be selfish for the time being or maybe longer, if necessary. And, if you are the trusty companion, this is the time to offer support like never before. Stay close, listen, and keep it simple.

You may decide to return as a group with your squad mates or, perhaps, with those Officers who fought alongside you. You may want to take your family. Just remember that whether someone died on the scene or not, that location is now sacred ground and if you feel the need to venture back, you should go. Something inside of you is calling you back. Embrace it. You may arrive and get hella pissed. Good! You may decide no matter what the circumstance, you are *never* going back again and that's just fine, too.

For a long list of reasons, the scene of my first shooting was significant for me. Those reasons are not important right now, but the area in which the shooting took place is. It is sacred ground. Not because I took a life, but because I survived it. The lady who owned the car that knucklehead broke into owned a trinket shop in that strip mall. I asked her if there was something in her store that I could mount on the wall next to the scene as a memorial, a little something for us both. We found a heart cut from a small piece of wood. That seemed appropriate. She helped me place it in a secure, but visible spot on the wall. We hugged and said a prayer of thanks for each other. That interaction brought me some peace.

There are many ways to restore or find peace, with or without going back to the scene. There are many spots around my city, in the area where I used to work that are memorialized, marking tragic scenes of fallen Officers. Oftentimes I drive past and give a shout out or whisper a quick prayer. Sometimes I stop and reflect for a bit. There is one sacred spot I pass by regularly, always touching my fingers to my lips and praying. I have left candles and mementos, including Matchbox® cars, belt keepers and even a box of toothpicks. And sometimes I don't ever go to the scene, but instead to the cemetery—occasionally both. If you choose not to go to either of these places, it does not mean that you do not care. Everyone grieves and deals with loss differently. They are never to be judged—ever! Remember that being happy, over time, particularly after suffering a loss, is **not** a betrayal of the fallen. We, the living, must carry on.

CHAPTER FORTY
Road to Recovery

I have seen a lot of death in my time, lots of destruction and so forth. I suspect it's for good reason that certain details remain suppressed deep in the recesses of my mind. My retirement date was set for April 17, 2018. Twenty years and I would be *free*. I had it all planned out. Apparently, God had other plans in place for me, far less remarkable than that of my colleague, the great David Glasser—Davey, as his mom likes to call him.

Looking back, **May 18, 2016** was the actual day I retired. I did my absolute best to recover, to make it back to some semblance of normal. I did that with the help of good people, a team that included:

- Shrinks
- Medical doctors
- Tac guys
- Training detail guys
- Squad mates
- Clergy
- Employee assistance

I sought them all—often and continuously. Unfortunately, the help came too late ... not too late for recovery, but too late for me to admit that I was a mess. I was behind the curve. My close friends kept saying, "Hey, man! We think you need help."

Nope. I'm good.

"No. You're not."

Oh yeah! I'm good. I promise that I am okay.

"Bullshit!"

I got called out and was forced to face my demons. Here's the thing: You **cannot** go 18 years in law enforcement, catching bad guys, seeing stuff that shakes people to their very foundation and believe that you are inherently okay. They call that denial ... straight up, no bullshit denial. I had made a comment, something about "hiding" on the street and the folks who knew me and, more importantly, cared about my well-being said, "Nope. Bullshit. You are **not** okay! And here are some ways to get fixed."

And I'll be damned, if it didn't work ... not always directly, but it gave me other avenues to explore and to "fix" myself. I started paying attention, too. I was tired of feeling lost and I desperately wanted to get back in the game. What was it, again, that took me out? Oh right! It was an ambush ... a gunfight ... an Officer down and another evil person that I was forced to kill. That made three, three evil people in my world who dared to try to kill me. And, of course, it wasn't just *my* world. In fact, I had very little to do with the reckless and suicidal decisions made by these animals. They were being led by the hand of Satan. All I did was pay attention in class and learn how to pull a trigger.

Did I ever think that I would be so adversely affected by the events of a shooting? Not nearly enough. Sure, I listened to the stories and true accounts of other Officers. I learned when and what I could, but it never actually sank in, not until it happened to me. It was only then that I could describe the emotions I was feeling after a supremely critical incident. And for those who have not had to experience it, I pray that you never do. Those who *have* will understand the meaning of that last sentence. Are we, as new Officers, curious to know what it is like to experience a gunfight? Killing another human being?

Of course!

It is to be expected. However, there is a wide range (WIDE RANGE!) of emotions that will absolutely follow, and this is far more impactful than shooting bad guys. A single critical incident can and will have some potentially unexplainable effects on your psyche and may not even manifest until years later. Now, multiply those times the number of traffic fatalities and stabbings and beat downs you experience and/or witness on the street and in court. If you think these things can't screw with your head, you are kidding yourself. Sure, you might get through a long career just fine, but those events need to be processed and released from within and often, lest you be left to manage severe symptoms of **post-traumatic stress**. Now there is a hot topic!

Opinions vary on the subject, depending on who you talk to. I have my own personal beliefs. However, it is, of course, biased and I will leave my opinions out. The fact is as first responders, we need a release. Each person must figure out what that release looks like. Soul search and/or chat with peers, if you have to. I don't care how you determine what that looks like. It needs to be done! Whether it's hiking, skydiving, playing the piano or playing tennis. Do something, anything, to get freed up regularly from the bad stuff. Again, from my tiny brain and humble opinion, I say that because I lost time. I lost friends and self-worth because I was ignorant and arrogant enough to believe that this couldn't touch me. No way!

Wrong again, Grasshopper!

Is it a fight? I'd say it is ... a big one! We, as an agency, lost 16 in the line of duty in my 20 years. That is in just my agency—alone. I submit, that I do not have an accurate count of Officers from the surrounding agencies, nor from across the country who made the ultimate sacrifice. However, I can tell you that the numbers are staggering. As I mentioned before, I have seen death. I have been to the funerals of many Officers, some I've known, some I never met and so my feelings run deeper than most. The last funeral I attended was especially profound because of my connection to the Officer and because of my direct involvement to the incident. Getting over these things can be a constant fight and you'd better be prepared for it.

The same is true for family, anyone at the other end of the telephone who might anticipate the dreaded call should be prepared to take it. At least six times in my career the call was made, *the call* that I was in some sort of trouble, not in trouble with the brass, but real life and death trouble. When a call like that is made, it is generally one of two incidents:

1. An Officer involved shooting

2. The Officer is in the hospital

Of course, that doesn't include all the incoming calls from friends and family when the news gets out that an Officer was injured, killed, or simply involved. Then you should expect your phone to be ringing off the hook.

Like most people, when a strange number pops up on your phone, you wonder whether or not to pick up. It's natural. However, do you want my advice? If your significant other is "on the job" and the telephone is ringing, you should take the call—every single time! Telemarketers be damned! You can always hang up on them. Okay. I am just kidding, but they know the drill. Seriously, take the call!

What if you ***don't*** take the call because you don't recognize the phone number and it happens to be a true emergency? What then? What if the caller doesn't try you back and you learn about the incident on the news or on social media?

Absolutely unacceptable!

Believe me when I say, seeing two uniformed Officers who you may or may not know approach your front door is the worst thing imaginable. However, as bad as that is, imagine the sheer blindsided feeling of getting the "Officer Down" notification from Facebook®, alongside a stupid photo someone posted of their dinner. Actually, **do not** try and imagine that at all. Instead, figure out a protocol to follow for when, God forbid, that phone call happens. Make sure it is something that makes sense for ***your*** family. It's unfortunate, but it's reality. It is the family version of the "what if" game that I mentioned earlier.

What follows the dreaded phone call, of course, is the unending commentary about what they, the "rumor millers," know about the incident. Cops are notorious for spreading rumors. They are the worst! There's a lot of hearsay, a lot of "I heard this," and "No. I was told that," or "My sister's fiancé knows a guy who works in the area and his boss said such and such."

Are you kidding me?

Are we are not going to try and help the other squad mates or the Officer's family or secure the scene if the opportunity presents itself? Instead, and let's be honest here, we are going to make some shit up because we think we "know" the Officer in question. You know the one, the Officer we don't like or respect, so we assume he/she did everything wrong. We have enough of a fight on our hands as it is in law enforcement, without adding fuel to the fire with unsolicited hearsay.

Please!

I can tell you without hesitation that those Officers on a critical incident scene have a difficult time remembering the facts … and they were there! How could anyone who was not there possibly have a clue what really happened? As family, do not take anyone's word for it.

Answer the phone!

CHAPTER FORTY-ONE
Critical Incident Debrief

Most agencies, as far as I know, have two types of mandatory debriefings. The first is the "Critical Incident Stress" type. This is where Officers have the opportunity to discuss their feelings and emotions and such. Sometimes this debrief is a recap of the event and sometimes it is a deeper discussion where Officers can open up about their feelings or just sit back and listen in a safe, confidential environment. It is designed as a roundtable and following a critical event, it can usually be very tough to sit through. Mental health experts are called upon to help and/or share experiences at these debriefings. In my opinion, I believe it is important that everyone involved in a critical incident take part.

The second type of mandatory debriefing is the "Tactical Debrief." This is where folks on the scene of a critical incident or those directly involved gather to discuss the more technical aspect of a scene. Facts are the key here. Therefore, all emotions should be left at the door. It is a time for thick skin and accountability.

In the Tactical Debrief, it is immediately apparent when someone is not willing to participate. They will either remain silent or not show up for it at all, which is fine. However, if you are summoned to one of these two types of debriefings and you do actually have the choice whether or not to attend, please, (please!) at least attend one of them, if not for yourself, for your partner or those involved. You never know who may need your input at one of these debriefings.

Yes, it's a big deal!

Personally, I was a little disappointed in my first CISM debrief following the first of my Officer-involved shootings. Not knowing the protocol, I asked if a friend could attend with me. My request was denied. I didn't know if it was department policy or what, but that "denial" ate away at me. It became my primary focus versus getting something useful out of the debriefing. I walked away without any valuable information or reason to help process the incident. This was *not* an effective way to proceed. These critical debriefs, I have learned, are two-fold:

1. They are designed to show how others handled the situation and, therefore, how policy dictates how or why things were handled in a particular way. This information is unlimited and can vary from ammunition load out to assigning a scribe for the Dispatcher or countless other topics.

2. They are designed to support others. *Your* presence may make someone else who was on the fence about going, **want** to be there. And if you are the one "on the fence," your peers should be made aware that you want and need their support and attendance. The other types of debriefs are as follows:

1. **Squad Only**: A lot of good can be done here. Remember, these are the folks you spend almost as much time with as your family, if not more.

2. **One-on-one**: Whether it's a squad mate, a clergy or a workout buddy, there is no limit as to who you confide in. The point is it's good to open up and share with someone. I caution against the chest-thumping "gung-ho" chats, at least in the beginning. However, everyone is built differently and maybe that is exactly what is needed at the time.

3. **Departmental/County Review Board**: This debrief usually happens a year or more later, depending upon the incident. This one can be tough for a variety of reasons, like having to relive the entire incident all over again, but this time in front of a whole lot of brass and civilians. You find yourself standing outside of a large room, waiting for your fate to be decided by people who were not even on the scene, discussing

what you did right and what you did wrong. The setting, as I have seen it, is usually an oversized room filled with dozens of people. There is usually a PowerPoint presentation depicting the scene. There is a roundtable of introductions and then the story is told by the Officer(s). Afterward, the Officer(s) are asked to step outside, while the remaining folks debate on whether or not the right decisions were made. It usually does not take very long. In my personal experience, around five or 10 minutes later, the Officer(s) are invited back into the room and the decision-makers share their findings. It can be a bit stressful, but it is something that must be done. It is usually very straight-forward and factual-based. I will say this; if you train the right way and act responsibly in the course of your duties, I can assure you that there will likely *not* be a problem with your actions. Trust me; everything will be alright.

ON A SIDE NOTE

#6807

My generation was advised to keep the mental, physical, and emotional toll of the job close to our vest. That is to say, we were told **not** to share our "day" as Officers with our families. It was the late 90s and it was law enforcement's universal answer to keeping our emotions in check. Why? The canned response was, "Because that's how we've always done it."

Like most organizations, law enforcement is a progressive entity or, at least, it should be. We must continue learning and pushing forward to survive this venture of crime fighting. One particularly aggravating issue, for me, personally, is what happens to Officers immediately following a critical incident. It used to be we would take these Officers to the nearest restaurant, pull up a seat and talk quietly—regain composure, if possible. It would be the time to gather a few facts from your boss, if he or she had any. Nowadays, these "debriefs" often happen in the back of MAC vans— Mobile Activity Command. The vans are great, but these things take time, an hour on average and a mobile unit doesn't provide great comfort or space. Plus, in today's society, we want and need to protect our Officers from negative publicity.

Yeah?

Here is the problem. Oftentimes, for lack of a better place, Officers involved in a critical incident are escorted into the backseat of a patrol car. Now, there are very few, if any places I can think of that are worse to put an Officer, someone who may clearly be under duress. Imagine, if you will, one of your Officers just got into a gunfight and was forced to shoot and kill someone and now you want to cram him into the backseat of a patrol car, the same cramped quarters you cram the shitheads of his world.

Are you kidding me?

Not to mention, there is probably very little air conditioning available, and except for the assigned supervisor—zero human contact. On top of which, the Officer gets to watch as his/her worried buddies arrive on scene, unable to reassure them that he/she is okay. I understand the dynamic and it's not always the way it is, but it still angers me when I see it happen. And, again, the canned response from upstairs is always the same, "That's how we've always done it."

That's not okay!

There are always better solutions. If a patrol car is all that you have, so be it. I say ask the Officer what he/she wants, needs, or prefers. It's about making your Officer as comfortable as possible. If you have all your gear and shit piled on the front passenger seat, move it out of the way, throw it on the ground, if you have to. **Do whatever is necessary to take care of your own.** Obviously, it is best to remove the Officer from the scene, assuming it is possible. We always advise the Officer that the investigation is ongoing, so we advise they not speak until their rep or the investigators give the okay ... or whatever policy dictates. And, of course, there are those more personal, if not important questions that should be asked: What can I bring you? Where would you be most comfortable? Have you contacted your family, and can I help with that?

Keep in mind ... this is not the time to overwhelm the Officer with unnecessary commentary. Keep it brief and basic. If the assigned supervisor is *not* CISM or a Department shrink, then avoid the "Are you okay?" type of questions and only have the trained staff approach. As a supervisor, I believe it is wise to get to know your people, so when that day does, in fact, come ... you are prepared to respond.

For example, if your Officer chews Green Skoal® or drinks Mountain Dew® or what have you, have someone go retrieve the goods. Of course, I'm not suggesting encouraging reckless behavior, like buying the Officer a bottle of brandy. However, if it's something he/she can do while on duty, I say, "What's the harm?" Denying comfort items could prove much worse in the long run. And, finally, don't ever, ever, EVER say to an Officer, "Good job, killer!" or any other foolish statement of the kind. For weeks and perhaps even months, emotions run high and those words, while seemingly harmless and innocent in nature, have no business following a critical incident. Such comments are inappropriate and can be confusing to the Officer. Support is what is needed most here. It's a different kind of fight.

CHAPTER FORTY-TWO
One Year Later

I was not on David's squad—same unit, different squad. So, when the time came for 2017 National Police Week in Washington D.C., a time to honor our fallen, David's squad invited me to attend. I believe the actual words were, "You're going and that's that!"

How do you argue that?

Humbled, I joined Dave's grief-stricken squad, along with a lot of family members, including children and some of the brass and fellow Officers who wanted to show their support. David's squad was the JV squad, younger guys mostly, at least compared to most of *my* squad. There was a lot of joking around about them being "young whippersnappers" and "babies." The fact is, and part of the reason for writing this particular story, is that they, as a squad, were the tightest I had ever seen. They were comprised of guys who truly cared about one another and who were friends … both on and off the street. I secretly envied them for that. I still do. And they wanted *me* to join them in D.C. What an honor! I felt like I was intruding, but the decision had been made even prior to my accepting.

Okay. So be it.

It was my first National Police Week, although it was not my first time in D.C. Words cannot describe the magnitude, not to mention the importance of attending this annual event. I had been encouraged to attend in years past, but I gave the same obligatory response that other Officers give, "Oh yeah! That sounds nice. I will go before I retire."

The fact is most of us will never attend, not unless the fallen is a close friend or squad mate. That's too bad. Knowing what I know now, I believe *everyone* needs to experience the profoundness of this event before it is your agency honoring one of your own. There is a deep-rooted feeling of despair, honor, and confusion when it's your agency attending as a host. That is to say that when it's your agency that has lost an Officer and has been officially invited to honor him or her, it hurts in places you didn't know you had. There are, however, certain perks to being a host agency, but I absolutely guarantee that there is not one Officer or agency that will ever want to attend for *that* reason.

We landed at Reagan International Airport on a dark, cold, and rainy night, befitting of the mood. There was a jam-packed itinerary, a long list of events that we were supposed to attend, including items we were to bring along for the journey, such as a suit, dress uniform, casual clothing, and comfortable shoes. The list of "don't forgets" was endless.

As the plane pulled into the terminal, the captain kindly made an announcement. "For those passengers who are not a part of the Glasser family, please remain seated until the family deplanes."

As we exited the jet way, we were met with a scene I will never forget as long as I live. It was a busy airport, virtually quiet. There were passengers all over the place, looking on as Law Enforcement Officers stood at attention, in tandem, creating a walkway. Peace Officers from the United Kingdom stood in full dress uniform, saluting us as we passed through. They had created a tunnel. I barely made it through without slipping and falling in a puddle of my own tears. It was going to be a long week.

Hold it together, man! Hold it together.

I called my shrink at the first opportunity, sharing every detail. The emotions were overwhelming. I'll be honest. Most of the week was a blur. Our itinerary included a lot of parades, gatherings, and early morning get-togethers, leaving very little time for sleep. Most of the events are considered tradition and are scheduled each and every year. Of course, there were special events that our brass chose, including a trip to the White House. That was cool! There were museums and lots and lots of sight-seeing. The most overwhelming of all was the candlelight vigil.

I have an incredible photograph of the candlelight vigil. It is virtually a sea of people holding candles on the National Mall. I show it to my audiences when I speak, a reminder to them that the world doesn't hate law enforcement as much as one might think. To look at this picture, one can see and believe that there are millions of people who love us.

Despite the unbelievable humidity, combined with donning my full-dress uniform, it was an honor to stand on the Capital Lawn during the President's speech. Now, I am not politically motivated. Mostly, I keep my opinions to myself. However, when the President of the United States mentions a fallen Officer's son by name, and then throws a baseball cap to the young boy in the crowd, well, I'll be the first to say, "That was awesome!" How many kids in the world will ever be able to say that?

Thank you, Mr. President!

We spent a lot of time tooling around on foot. One of the coolest things I have ever seen was when Officers from different agencies around the country laid out their badges on a table for a photo op. Had I been a bit savvier, I would have taken more opportunities to do this. I do have one photograph that I will cherish forever though. It is totally cool!

As expected, there was also a fair amount of drinking and partying going on. This, at times, was tough. Because there was a lot of alcohol involved, it always led to toasting the fallen, which then led to storytelling and, ultimately, a lot of crying.

Tough times. Tough fight.

When we got to the memorial wall for the first time, I stood in awe. I was overwhelmed. Its whole reason for being was to honor the beautiful and tragic tales of our fallen heroes. I had never seen anything like it. Again, *everyone* should see this for themselves.

As a family, blood and blue, we walked down the long corridor, determined to find David's name as soon as possible. For one, we wanted to honor him and two ... we wanted to see if it was real, if Dave had really been taken from us so soon. As it turned out, it was real. We found his name carved in stone and those etchings don't lie. So, we took turns placing flowers, cards, and prayers next to his name. And with pencil led and paper, we captured the etching of his name to take home. I lost count how many etchings I brought home, but there were dozens. In the week that we were there, we visited the site as a group three or four more times. It was emotional, of course, but nice.

BROUGHT TO MY KNEES

#6807

I have no idea what night it was, but I received a phone call midway through the week. It was nine o'clock. I was tired, fighting the change in climate. The dense air was doing a number on my head and body.

"Hey, man! We're at the bar ... drinking. You need to join us!"

I declined at first, but then decided I needed to go have a drink with my friends. Three of them were Officers who had made the journey to honor another of our fallen. Incidentally, he was also a friend of mine. I had no idea these guys were in town, so the least I could do was join them in celebration of life, honoring our fallen friends. After about an hour or two of telling stories, toasting, and hugging it out, we headed down to the wall on foot. We were aimlessly walking around town. I had no idea this would turn out to be a life-altering event for me.

Two of my friends, a husband and wife, veered off toward another section of the wall where one of his squad mates had his name etched in 2013 after having given the ultimate sacrifice. Now *there* was a true story of heroism! My other friend and I made our way to David's sacred place. There was hardly a word spoken between us. She stopped briefly, said her peace, and then walked away, allowing me to sit alone. She must have known I needed that.

You know who you are. Thank you.

It was the perfect temperature, nice and cool and very quiet where I was. It felt very, very peaceful. I was completely alone with David for the first time, which was kind of strange, since every other visit I made had been packed with people. *That* must have been the difference it made for me to let down my guard. I sat quietly and reflected, recounting the event which had been crowding my mind, despite my best efforts to push it aside. I sat, wondering how I had ended up there. Why me? Why David? What was this doing to *his* family? I decided there was no room for negative thoughts, not on that night. I smiled at the idea that he was ready, ready to give up his life for his beliefs. That thought made me feel warm and safe.

After about 15 minutes or so, I decided it was time to go. I knelt and ran my fingers over the letters carved in cold limestone—David Glasser. The next thing I knew, I got knocked on my butt. I was crying uncontrollably, like never before. It was no less than 18 years' worth of tears. I was on my knees weeping and begging and cursing and denying and unable to gain control. Finally, after another 20 minutes, I was able to collect myself. I fumbled to my feet. Aimlessly, I walked toward the opposite side of the wall where my friend was waiting. She had obviously been crying, too. Our eyes met. It was a look of recognition. We both know why we were there.

"Are you alright," she asked.

"Yes. I …"

I got halfway through my response before the flood gates burst open—again! It was another 30 minutes, the two of us bawling together, asking the same question over and over again.

"Why?"

It was a question we both knew we would never get the answer to, but this is how it is for survivors and mourners. I only hope that someday the answers will come.

After our little crying session, my friend returned to her best buds and I made a beeline for my hotel. With all that crying out of the way, I felt like running, which is kind of funny. I sprinted a whole mile in blue jeans and boots. It felt good, so good that I even laughed to myself. It was refreshing to find some humor in all of this, which I think Dave would have appreciated, if not wanted.

CHAPTER FORTY-THREE
The Morning After

I got up the next morning with a newfound outlook on life, as if a reset button had been mercifully pushed. It came out of nowhere. Maybe it was the time alone with David the night before. Maybe it was sharing stories with friends. Maybe God, in all His wisdom and mercy, finally reached me. I have no idea, but I was finally feeling *really* good after one full year of sulking and struggling. All the bad stuff had been released. It was epic, a feeling of relief that was virtually tangible. Naturally, I wanted to share this newfound energy with someone. There was only one person I could think of who needed it as much, if not more than me and that was my supervisor buddy.

David's squad had each other to lean on, but he and I were outsiders, not in a bad way, just not a part of the original family—so to speak. We did, however, end up becoming a part of that family a little later, which, I might add, was a huge blessing for us both. This supervisor, a good friend of mine and a good man, blamed himself for losing David. In other words, he "ran the show," that fateful day, creating the perfect plan, not knowing that Satan would step in and ruin it for us all. He was

262

devastated by the loss of another man, someone to whom he referred to as, "one of his kids," even if it was only for that one call.

The next morning, we are all gathered outside of the hotel lobby. I spotted my supervisor buddy and immediately went up to him.

"Hey, man! You've got to hear this story," I said, smiling. "So, I was out last night …"

The immediate vibe I got was less than interested. His expression said, "Nope! Shhh … I don't want to know. Stop talking."

Out of respect, he let me finish. However, I could see he wanted no part in my revelation, which I, in turn, respected.

It is your fight for you to fight.

We spent another full day of sightseeing, ending with a special invitation to the bar. This was the first opportunity for Kristen, David's widow, to join us. I was definitely not planning on missing that one. So, there we were, chatting and drinking and such. There were a lot of hugs. Overall, it was a pretty positive atmosphere. Everything was going quite well until I got a phone call.

"Chris, can you come to the wall? He's not well."

I dropped my drink and sprinted back to the wall. It was yet another quiet, cool night. The wall was mostly empty. My supervisor buddy's amazing, sweet wife was sitting on a bench, just opposite the wall.

She was curled up in a ball, crying her eyes out.

Oh my God what happened?

I rounded the corner, just in time to see my friend on his knees punching the wall. In a fit of anger, he yelled and then ripped his shirt off and threw it at the limestone memorial.

Okay. We are buds. I can handle this.

I quietly knelt down next to him, letting him rant for a few minutes longer. I opened my mouth to speak, but he was already jacked up. He plainly wanted no part of me. I stood to my feet. Since subtlety was not working, I started yelling at the top of my lungs. He responded in kind. Before long it was a screaming match, a verbal brawl that turned into a game of blame. We both blamed ourselves for everything that went wrong.

"Fuck you!" he shouted. "You don't understand. *I* was in charge."

"No," I exclaimed. "Fuck you! *I* let it happen! I missed the guy in the van!"

"It was my plan!" he cried.

"I was the first one on scene!" I screamed.

"I'm a supervisor. It's my responsibility!"

"I was the scout. I failed!" I shouted.

This went on for a few minutes, until it finally dawned on me that the only direction this fight was going was down. With the two of us verbally slugging it out, attempting to gain ground over *who* let David die, we were getting nowhere. This was not working, so I grabbed him around the neck and pulled him in close. It was this move that ultimately and profoundly changed this spiraling event … a*nd my life*!

"No! No! No!" he cried, fighting back.

That's when it hit me like a sledgehammer to the temple—again! It brought it all back. The last time he and I were in this type of scuffle was on the scene. With that flashback, I came unglued. A year had passed, but I was still emotional about this. However, this was different. It was violent, uncontrollable, and raw emotion. Tears were flowing like I did not even think was humanly possible.

Damn it! I just got my head on straight last night!

It instantly hit me that this was no longer about me. I had made my way off *my* ledge. My buddy was still on his. There was no panic for me this time, just straight shooting. Harsh as they were, the words that spewed out of my mouth were from the heart, but they were harsh, nonetheless. I couldn't tell you what I said, but I know they were tough to hear. It was probably something to the effect of, "Shut the fuck up and get back in the game! It's time to face the fact that there was nothing … **nothing** any of us could have done to stop this from happening. Do you fucking understand me?!?!"

The words were so harsh that he shut down almost immediately. All that was left were tears. It must have been a pretty good screaming match because I suddenly realized we were not alone. There were about eight other guys gathered around, watching our verbal fistfight. They seemed highly concerned that we were *not* okay and likely concluding that they might be forced to do something about it.

"Hey man! You guys okay," one of the bystanders asked.

Of course! Why would you think otherwise?

It was super, super healing at the end of it all, but I would not wish to repeat it or the next hour spent with fellow Officers from all over the country, trading stories about how and why they landed in D.C. Believe me. Each story was worse than the last. It was stunning, to say the least. By the time it was over, my supervisor buddy only had one thought.

"Damn! I'm hungry! How about you?"

A giant smile came over both of our faces.

You know what, man? We are going to be alright.

It was two o'clock in the morning in downtown D.C., not exactly a Barcalounger in the firehouse.

Just kidding, guys!

My buddy and I walked for hours, ate some food, and basically had a ball. All things considered, it could have turned out very different.

Truth: It was precarious at best, but we were okay. We were 10 feet tall again and the spirit of Dave was flowing through every inch of us.

Hell yeah!

I woke up the next morning feeling happy. It was kind of funny when I saw my buddy outside. I approached him, fully intending on revisiting the glory of our collective revelation the night before.

Yeah. I got shunned.

"Back the fuck off," he said. "Don't hug me! I am pissed at you!"

Well! A fine morning to you, too, fucker!

Almost immediately, he admitted to feeling pretty good, but that he was pissed that I *made* him battle through it.

Hee hee hee

I took that as a compliment!

Love you, man. I am glad you are okay.

CHAPTER FORTY-FOUR
Giving Battle

I had the distinct honor of meeting a Green Beret while in D.C. during Police Week. He was a Warrior and an all-around good guy. The more I come to know these "types" of guys, the more I appreciate how humble this particular Green Beret was on the day that I met him.

Yes. I said it ... these "types" of guys.

I'm talking about guys who go into battle, Warriors who do and see the unimaginable. They are blown up, shot up and all while tending to their wounded and dead. They are the ones who refuse to leave the battlefield, putting aside their own wounds that need patching up. This gentle giant of a man had, in his time, cried out the Warrior's chant, "I must get back into the fight to help my men! They are still out there!"

Knowing that about this former Green Beret made it all the more humbling that he wanted to hear *my* story. This was significant for me because when I hear what these brave soldiers did and do on the battlefield, in comparison to what I did every day out on the street, I can't help but feel less than worthy. Not worthless, mind you … just not in the same league of hero.

When I reached the end of *my* own personal war story, the Green Beret recapped for me and then asked, "What will be your fate when you return to the street?"

I wasn't about to question this guy. No way! However, deep down I was thinking to myself, *Do we have to go there?*

"You mentioned," he continued. "Before you shot the dog, you had a couple of close calls, and then you shot your first bad guy. You counted two or three times before you pulled the trigger for real. And then next was a rifle shooting … followed by a gunfight."

I had no idea where he was going with this recount of events, but I held fast to every word.

"Yes," the Green Beret continued. "You are going to get shot. Look at it, but here is the reality. **You are a fucking a Warrior!** Right? You are four-for-four, and you are not done with your time on the street, one of *the* most violent areas in the country. And **you will not stop out of fear** or because of the brass or for any other reason. Am I right?"

At that point, he was screaming at me.

Jesus! Okay. Yes!

"You're gonna get shot," he shouted. "You're gonna fucking kill your opponent and your fire department is one of the best, so they will fix you up. You are going to be just fine. Do you understand me?"

Hell yeah!

Who the hell is going to argue with a former Green Beret? Besides that, who would know better than a Special Forces guy with multiple combat tours under his belt? I took an epic verbal beating, of sorts. It filled me with a whole lot of pride, fear, and a burning to get back to my work on the street. It also forced me to reinvent my sense of courage, although it took me a while to find comfort back in the saddle. I will never forget that day or the time spent with my new friend, the Green Beret.

You know who you are.

Despite another 18 months on the street, I survived a 20-year career, physically unscathed. Well, that's not entirely true. There was a broken ankle, a broken wrist, a hernia, a spider web fracture of the knee, near-death dehydration, but I am happy to report there were no bullet holes. That's something! And because I'm stubborn as all get-out, I never left the street after being injured. It beat the alternative, burning through sick time or riding the desk or answering phones. Suck it up, I say!

CHAPTER FORTY-FIVE
Breaking Point

When I heard the news I was devastated. Bane, a Belgian Malinois with a heart of gold, had a work ethic better than most Officers with only two legs. He did his job well and, on that fateful day, he did not make it home. The dog died a hero. My best friend and fellow Officer was Bane's handler and this deadly deployment would prove to be a major setback for me, a stumbling block that would ultimately lead to my early retirement.

When I got the call confirming that it was my best friend who was involved, I had a much overdue meltdown. Very much like losing Dave, it was way too much to handle. I knew my friend had been through a long list of painful personal issues and this was the last thing he and his family needed. It was the last thing any of us needed. My issue came when I got back to the office. Stupidly, I let my emotions take over and I literally cleaned out my desk, packed up my stuff in a box and left. On my way out I snapped at my boss. "I'm done with this shit!"

It was a Monday, and I took the rest of the week off. I told my boss I had planned to take some time off and he basically agreed.

"Alright," he said.

I knew he didn't *really* approve of me bailing out the way I did, but then again there were things he didn't know about me, personal things that made this loss hit hard. So, over the next few days I called into work to let them know I wasn't coming in, just as I was supposed to. What I did not do, however, was answer the return phone calls to confirm that I was alright. I admit. It was a mistake and downright selfish of me, but I had a total "fuck it" attitude and flat out did not want to be bothered, let alone discuss my mental state. That did not sit well with either of my supervisors.

When I returned to work the following Monday, I was called into a meeting that ultimately forced my hand into retirement. I was told that because I refused to tell my supervisors what was going on with me, they decided I was not fit for street duty. So, for the next several weeks I was assigned a desk, pending the outcome of a decision to be made by upper management. I was not surprised, but then again, I was sort of taken aback. As supervisors, they had decisions to make. I understood then and, to this day, I still understand. Like it or not, as a low to mid-level employee, I was a number. However, I will admit, my department did do a decent job of taking care of me. And I certainly appreciated that, but they'd had enough of me by that point. This was where things got sticky and, for the record, very ugly.

I took my licks and stuck it out on desk duty for five weeks, five grueling weeks. At one point I was reduced to scraping the department barbeque grill. For a guy who can't sit still for very long and who hates being trapped indoors, this was devastating. It was the first and only time in my career that I had ever been in that type of "disciplinary" situation. During that time, I received an email stating that I was required to get a physical clearance before going back to full-duty.

Okay ... no biggie.

I got clearance from the doctor and reported back to work, on top of which I had been openly seeing a shrink on my own time. I had documentation showing I was fit for duty from her, as well. I was called into another formal meeting in the commander's office. It was the commander, both of my first line supervisors and me. We were there to discuss my previous actions and, ultimately, my fate with the department.

Fair enough.

I figured they deserved an explanation, and I was ready to give it.

"Do you know why you're here?" the commander asked.

"No, sir, I do not."

"Your boss didn't explain this meeting to you," he continued.

"No."

I don't remember his exact words, but my supervisor said something to the effect of him not being aware of the meeting either.

I'm Sorry, but that's fucking bullshit!

Anyway, the meeting continued, pointing out the mistakes I had made. I listened openly, taking it all in.

"Who gave you the authorization to get a medical clearance without permission," the commander inquired.

"I was sent an email that requested I get it done, sir," I replied.

I am not the brightest of folks, but I do know a few things. For instance, when I get an email that is addressed to me, carbon copying my sergeant and human resources personnel, I pay attention … especially when there is no name listed in the "sender" slot. I got suspicious, suspicious enough to print out a copy of said email, just in case.

"And who sent this email?"

"I don't know, sir. There was no return address to speak of."

I had a printed copy of the email with me, as a backup plan, but never needed it. After a few more questions relating to my well-being, the big boss came out with it.

"Okay. Here it is," he said. "I know you have been through hell, especially in the last few years. I expect that you would certainly be screwed up and … that's alright. I know you're a great and talented Cop. Now, go get a clearance from the city shrink. Get back in this game and do me a favor. Next time, just handle shit better … alright?"

His speech gave me a flashback of my academy sergeant's little spiel regarding the reloads. Suddenly, I had a giant smile on my face.

"Yes, sir," I exclaimed. "Thank you for your support and for believing in me. I promise I won't let you down."

I seriously wish I could have been a fly on the wall after I was dismissed and asked to close the door behind me, but that was another of those "above my pay grade" situations. So, after all was said and done, I did make it back to full-duty and I regained my confidence before calling it quits. However, deep down, I knew I was done. Truth be told, I had no choice but to prove to myself that I could still be out there chasing bad guys, but it was also abundantly obvious that I had no business on my particular squad anymore. I was burned out for good in the law enforcement community.

I remember when I was fresh out of the academy. I would ask my sergeant if I could come in for overtime or just work for free.

"Boss," I begged. "I love this shit! I'll work on my own time. I swear. I can't get enough."

"Not possible," he barked. "Trust me when I tell you, take your time and enjoy your days off. You will have plenty of time to chase bad guys.

How right he was! I took his advice, carefully monitoring how much I gave to my work and, more importantly, how much I gave at home. I learned to leave the Cop hat at work and wear the civilian hat where it counted. Despite all my efforts to maintain the much-needed balance, I still got clobbered and it all came to an ugly head on April 17, 2018. Twenty years later ... to the day!

My actual retirement day, as well as the retirement "party," was quick and easy, except for my last call. That was tough and there were tears. I remember listening to several minutes of, "Thank you!" and "We'll miss you!" and so forth. It was pretty amazing!

Not long after leaving the department, I got a bit stir crazy. I knew I would end up going back to work, but in what capacity? I did have a brand-new, practically tangible feeling of happiness. I was relaxed and had never felt so free. Don't get me wrong. I'm not advising anyone to seek retirement too early, but retiring was the best thing I ever did for my overall well-being. I soon found my dream job ... training Police recruits in San Diego, California. Not only had I always dreamed of living by the beach, but all my knowledge and experience could now be shared with those coming up in the ranks behind me and, even better than that, there would be no more getting shot at.

What a concept!

This book, combined with my retirement and newfound purpose, means that I have accomplished some major milestones and, more importantly, have lived to talk about it. Unfortunately, for a lot of my friends, that is not the case. So, in memory of all the fallen Officers, I offer my thoughts and prayers. And to those brave souls still bearing the weight of the badge while out saving the world, I offer my guidance, my wisdom and, of course, my very best. **GOD BE WITH US ALL**.

CHAPTER FORTY-SIX
Delilah

When I retired, I was not given the option to keep Delilah, my trusty sidekick. She would continue the journey in law enforcement without me and, so I included this letter, written for me by my favorite precinct desk aide for the next Officer who worked with her. Oorah, lady!

Letter to the Officer now assigned to this rifle

This COLT 6920 was mine. I was entrusted with her care, and most importantly, to utilize her in protecting others, enforcing the law, and making sure that the threats were stopped, and justice was served. I have strong and powerful memories attached to this rifle. I used it twice in my Police career to stop those threats. One of those incidents came with the ultimate high price. I used it on September 20, 2013 in a 998 to help put an end to a felony flight suspect who gave us no other choice. The rifle did its job, and I did mine. My attachment might sound crazy, but this rifle, my "Delilah" as I nicknamed her, became a part of me. She was my partner. She never failed me. On May 18, 2016, Officer David Glasser #8144 gave his life for this city and for his friends. I was there. I saw David fall and the next five seconds felt like five years. There wasn't time to think—only react. This rifle, once again, did not fail me. She reacted with me, became an extension of me. Within those five seconds, the evil-doer that took David away from us, moments earlier, now lie motionless himself. Delilah's rounds had found their target. This rifle stopped a Cop killer.

Now that I'm retiring from the department, I pleaded to take Delilah with me. I would pay any price for the unbreakable bond I have with this rifle. The memories and the meaning I share with this vital part of my law enforcement career are so powerful, but it looks like I need to let go … let go of Delilah and let go of this chapter in my life. I am passing the torch to you, Officer. I am passing this rifle to you. I am entrusting you with her care. Pick your own name for it if you choose. Keep it clean and safe. Stay up to date on training and qualifying. I know that you know all of this, but I just need to say it. Remember to stay focused and deploy it when absolutely needed. And deploy it in David Glasser's memory … with both love and vengeance. I am asking that you please keep David's badge shroud with this rifle at all times. And I ask you to stay safe and get home to your family at the end of every shift. Thank you for hearing me out.

LOVE YOU … from David Glasser's lips to God's ears.

Chris Hoyer #6807

CHAPTER FORTY-SEVEN
I am a Survivor

I am a survivor. This is not a statement or a topic I take lightly. In fact, sometimes it is tough to talk about. The truth is I never considered the possibility of having to **survive** this career, at least not in the "normal" sense of the word. Surviving gunfights, car crashes and burning buildings, all the typical Hollywood stuff that we think about when we decide to give this career a go is one thing. However, what does it mean to "survive" the end of your career? What does that look like? They did not mention that in the brochure. I am, of course, talking about financial security. Money is (or can be) an issue. It is, however, an easy fix with a little pre-planning. And then there is health and fitness. Statistically-speaking, we Officers tend to die five to six years after retirement. However, nowadays, those numbers are changing. We are not dying like we used to after retirement. Why is that?

In my opinion, it is because we have recognized the usefulness of mental preparation and have taken steps to ensure we are better prepared than past generations—physically, mentally, and yes, even emotionally.

With preparedness, I believe as Officers we can overcome just about any one critical incident. And trust me when I say, there will be plenty. Let us not recount those just yet.

What makes "surviving" difficult is the culmination of these critical events over time. For the most part, we sock them away, temporarily compartmentalize them in order to survive the next call, until one day … BAM! You are steamrolled, blind-sided by all the bad stuff!

If you are like me, or at least how I *used* to be, this job can oftentimes consume you. It starts off great and can be lots of fun, but over time it can become a burden. I figured out that there *must* be a release, something (anything) productive to escape the job and all that goes with it, including the daily grind, the angry people, the frustrated store owners, the heartbroken car crash victims and so on. Oh … and let's not forget the boss breathing down your neck. Trust me when I say, it will all catch up to you if you don't find an escape.

For me, my attitude changed when I started butting heads with my boss. I started asking myself more and more frequently, "Why am I doing this? The city does **not** take good care of me, at least not well enough to take a bullet for it. And the brass doesn't care about me."

So why am I breaking my back?

As time wore on, that was my attitude. Unfortunately, I have seen that same bad attitude happen a lot sooner in some Officers' careers, which is an absolute shame because that is going to be one hell of a long fight for those people. I truly believe that the lack of discipline in today's society and in our decision-makers' approach to job-related stress is going to make matters worse. For instance, allowing Police recruits and Officers alike to take these so-called "stress time outs."

Excuse me?

You can't handle getting yelled at in training, so you need to take a break? What the hell do you think is going to happen on the street or on the battlefield in real time? There are no time outs! What are you going to do? Pull out your pockets and sit on the fence for five minutes? It doesn't work that way. The problem is not that guys can't handle stress these days. The problem is *how* they handle stress.

I know. I know. I can already hear the disapproving groans.

I'm sorry. Actually, I'm not sorry because this is not how we protect our Warriors going into battle—on the street or in a foreign war zone. It comes down to muscle memory, folks. Muscle memory will keep our Warriors alive or it will surely get them killed. Let me explain. If you allow a kid to take a "stress time out" in training and then come real time when Bubba the giant, a threat wielding a shovel comes at him, hellbent on destruction, how do you think muscle memory will play a part here? If a recruit trains to take a "time out" when he is stressed, then combat-related stress is going to be a problem because you can't turn away from an actual threat, put your head down and wait until the stressor passes.

Yeah! Try that in real life, partner.

My point is this: I had a minimal amount of stress inoculation in my academy, which I thought was a bit weak. I am not taking a single thing away from the staff, but I believe there should have been more to prepare me for the stress of real time. I mean, if you cannot handle the stress of being beat down in a controlled environment, how are you going to manage the real deal? If you train to deal with the stress early on, face it head on, time and time again, I believe you have a better shot at survival when you actually encounter the bad stuff. It's not going to be easy, but it is a good fight, nonetheless. Enough said.

CHAPTER FORTY-EIGHT
You are a Warrior

In 2016 I started speaking to select groups about my experiences. Since then, I have been blessed with the opportunity to speak publicly across the country about my 20-plus years in law enforcement. It is both an honor and a privilege, something I don't take for granted. However, I will say that the first time I flew across these great United States to speak in a medium-sized city in the southeast, I thought I was King Shit. It was a two-day event, recruits on day one and in-service/family on day two. A colleague introduced me to this life, and I am very thankful for that chance.

I will never forget the very first time I was introduced to my audience. It was a moving and a humbling experience. My introduction went something like this: "Over here we have Officer Hoyer. He will speak about his four shootings in great detail and surviving a career. Oh ... and he is four-for-four on his kills."

Now, I do not embarrass easily ... nor am I shy, but when I was met with a standing ovation to that introduction, I was moved.

284

No kidding.

I stood there shocked, mouth open, thinking to myself, *Stop …
please. Trust me. I am nothing special. I am just a regular dude.* I really
did not know what to think of it. I admit the applause was confidence-
building. Yet, I still had no idea what would be required of me in this
particular "spotlight" and. that I would need all the confidence I could
muster to carry out the work ahead of me.

After a couple of days delivering my presentation, folks in the
audience started approaching me with questions. I was prepared for that, as
I had been speaking locally, having delivered my presentation a couple of
dozen times up to that point. However, I was stopped dead in my tracks on
this occasion. The truth is I never thought much about it. I was just telling
my story. The audience presented the usual battery of questions: How
many rounds did you fire? What is it like to kill? Do you have nightmares?
As a Cop, those are the questions I had grown accustom to answering. It
wasn't until that day in August of 2017 when a young man approached me
that I was thrown for a loop.

He was small in stature, young-looking. He practically whispered
when he spoke. He was dressed in detective-type clothing—unassuming.

"Excuse me, sir. Can I talk with you a little?"

I sensed apprehension in his voice, but I could see sadness in his eyes. I could tell he needed more from me than knowing whether or not I suffered nightmares. It seemed he was looking for guidance of some sort. This was new for me.

Be cool, Hoyer! Whatever you do, do not let this kid down.

I was still on high from having just presented to my biggest audience yet, so my response may have come off a little too eager.

"Heck yeah, man! What's up? How you doing? Are you okay?"

I'm sure he was thinking, *Shut up, asshole! I need to speak.* Luckily, I was not so obnoxious that he changed his mind.

"I was just wondering, if you could maybe help me a little," he whispered.

"Absolutely, my friend!" I replied. "What's up?"

"Well, I'm having a hard time deciding if I chose the right career and I'm wondering if I should continue on or quit. You see, we just lost another Officer."

"I'm sorry, man. That is just about the worst thing to happen in this profession."

I did not ask for details, but rather let him continue.

"Yeah," the young man said, clearing his throat. "He wasn't the first for me. There have been three. I lost an academy mate, a squad mate and now my partner."

In my mind, I was thinking this kid had to have had at least 12 to 15 years of experience under his belt to have lost three fellow Officers. That was rough.

"Oh my God, man! I cannot imagine. I am so sorry to hear that."

I was desperately searching for the right response.

Is there a right response?

"How much time on do you have with your department?" I asked.

"Two and a half years, sir."

Are you kidding me? Just two and a half years?

Panic set in.

Someone please help me.

Nope. It was my turn in the driver's seat—Mister Public Speaker, savior dude with a story to tell and a message to sell. It was my choice to be here.

Step up, man!

I had no idea what I needed to say or what this kid needed to hear. What do I tell him?

Yeah, man! It'll be fine. Just move forward. Don't worry. This shit won't ever happen again. Yeah. Let me rethink that.

In the meantime, I took a deep breath—combat breath.

Thanks, again, Lt. Colonel Grossman for that little reminder.

"That's quite stunning," I said. "Were all three in the line of duty?"

"Two of the three were."

How can I spin this?

"How long did it take you to get hired on?" I asked.

The look on this kid's face said, *What the fuck difference does* **that** *make?*

Nevertheless, he played along.

"About six months, sir."

"Yeah," I said. "It was about the same for me. How long is your academy out here?"

"About six months."

"That's long. Ours is just over four months," I answered, making sure not to add any more useless information than I had to. "What about field training?"

"Pretty much the same," he shrugged. "Six months. Sometimes it gets extended, of course."

Make your point, ass-head!

I nodded, posturing myself a little. Although I'm sure I was as visibly uncomfortable as he was.

"Did you sit through my whole presentation?"

"Yes, sir," he said. "I did."

"… and my partner's, too?"

"Yes."

"Right on," I smiled. "Thank you for that! So, you have been in the audience for close to four hours. Correct?"

"Close to it … yes."

"So, then, tell me this," I exclaimed. "How long did it take you to decide to come speak to me?

"I would say it was not long after your introduction."

"I see … and how long before you made it up here?"

"Three hours and change, I guess," he replied

Here comes the rub.

"Do you know what that was?"

"No," he replied, shaking his head with a blank look that was likely mirroring my own.

Again, I was new at this.

"That was a fight," I breathed.

"Sir?"

"You sat in the audience for over three hours and fought through a plan to share your story with me—a complete stranger. ***That's*** a fight. And I do not care how comfortable you thought you would be with me; it was no less a fight! It took you six months to get hired, six more months of training and six more months on the street. You, son, are a fighter!"

At that point my voice was elevated.

"You have lost three friends in almost as many years on the force, but have you quit?"

"No."

"You know why?" I barked. "Because you're a fighter ... goddamn it! You fought to get hired. You fought through the academy. You fought through FTO, and you fought for this career! You fought to carry on after you lost friends and you will continue to fight because you are a Warrior! Do you understand me? **Warriors face evil and they carry on**!"

I was just about screaming at him. He was fighting back tears and, truth be known, so was I.

"You are a warrior and that is that," I said, lowering my voice. "If you were going to quit, you would have by now. Now back to your question: Should you quit? That is *your* decision, my brother. Here are a couple things to think about. We know that you have Warrior's blood. However, there is absolutely no shame, whatsoever, in leaving this profession. Do you understand? You have earned the right and respect to walk away from this life with your head held high ... high and proud. Do you understand?"

The young man nodded.

"But here's something else to think about," I added. "What if the time comes when *you* are on this stage telling *your* story? There may be some kid out there who will need to hear your story and learn of your strength, gain an understanding of what you have endured and your ability to keep going. Do you want to let an Officer in need down, knowing what you know? An Officer looking for guidance, someone who may give up a rewarding career because he never got the answers he needed? *That* is your fight, too. There is a reason you are still here, a reason you chose to come today and a reason you chose to share your story with me."

I don't know who was more shocked with my sudden spur of inspiration, the young man or me. Graciously, he shook my hand and thanked me. As Law Enforcement Officers, we don't always know exactly when we make a difference. We just hope that we do. On that day, I knew I had made a difference and it felt good. I take a tremendous amount of pride in that. Before the young man turned to leave, I asked him one more question.

"Do me a favor. Take my information down. If and when you are on the fence or you need a shoulder or even a punching bag, reach out to me. Deal?"

He smiled.

I never did hear from him, but I understand that he is still a productive member of his department.

Good fight, Warrior! You know who you are!

CHAPTER FORTY-NINE
The Badge

In August 2017, I, along with some special colleagues, had the great privilege of being a guest of honor to the one and only Lieutenant Colonel Dave Grossman. He is an amazing individual, not to mention incredibly humble, generous and, obviously, highly intelligent. I have always been a fan of his and have read each and every one of his best-selling books. It's kind of funny because when I am reading alone, I get so into it that sometimes I will shout out loud, "Yes! I know *exactly* what you mean!"

Oh wait! Did anyone hear that?

He is spot on with his analysis of combat recounting and preparation. By the time I saw him speak live for the first time, I had a fair amount of law enforcement experience under my belt. I definitely paid attention to his words and to his stories, but did not really have the aptitude yet to appreciate all that he was saying—if that makes sense. I did, however, apply one life-changing tactic to my tool kit and that was **tactical breathing**. The first time I deployed this tactic, I was a bit skeptical, but I had nothing to lose. Shoot! He is a scholar, so maybe (just maybe!) he knows what he's talking about. Well, damned if it didn't work so well throughout the course of my career that I was often accused of being *too* calm on the radio.

Wait. What?

I was using it so regularly during stressful situations that I rarely got excited, which made it a huge benefit because when I *did* get excited, the common response from dispatch was, "Oh shit! If *he's* screaming, it *must be* a big deal! Send the cavalry!"

In his presentation, Dave Grossman told the story of a young Green Beret he met and the request he made. This story is *worth* mentioning. It was life-altering for me, and it just might be for you, too.

During an appearance, a young Warrior approached Grossman and asked him for a favor. "Will you tell your Police audience to remember that they are the home-front Warriors here in the states? I cannot protect my family while fighting a war 8,000 miles away. Tell them, please, not to let the bad guys hurt my family while I'm gone."

Writing these words brings tears to my eyes even now.

When I heard this story, all I could think was, *You, a pillar of strength, a Green Beret Warrior representing the best-of-the-best is asking us, law enforcement, to aid you?* The pride and responsibility I felt gave me the sense of a warm blanket. There was no other way to see it. It was a responsibility, one that I took seriously. In fact, the idea that this Green Beret depended on us to protect his family and the families of those like him, made me even *more* proud to say that I was a Police Officer. From that day forward, I carried out my duty with steadfast resolve. And I must say out loud to that brave Green Beret, "Thank *you*! Keep fighting! We got your six."

I had the opportunity to sit down alone with Dave. I discussed my career and my survival or at least my *attempts* at both. When I asked him if I could quote him during my own public speaking events, his response was something to the effect of, "My stuff is for everyone. If you mention it to someone else and it saves a life, I'd be honored if you would."

Did you just say that to me?

You know you are a total rock star, right?

I am the one blessed by your presence and knowledge.

While we're on the subject of pride, it is important that I say something about the badge. Maybe I am nutty, but here goes. When I discovered my true calling within the Department, I knew for sure life behind the badge would be home for me.

NET SQUAD

#6807

When I made it to NET Squad (Neighborhood Enforcement Team), there was, of course, a whole new sense of pride. So much so that I spent 16 years with this squad and, although I tried out for a couple other details, I *knew* it was home for me. Basically, we were still patrol—half patrol, half plain clothes, half catchall squad for Cops who didn't know who else to call. My joke was always, "When Cops don't know who to call … they call us." It was a little more training, a lot more freedom and a hell of a lot more fun! Plus, our uniform was jeans, a t-shirt, my badge fastened to a chain around my neck and no radio calls.

Oh, heck yeah! Sign me up.

Of course, being out of uniform was on a semi-rotating basis, but I was still just as happy in a marked car. When it came to uniforms, I didn't really have a problem until new uniforms were approved— pajama uniforms. There was some resistance to this new outfit, there still is to this day, but after a year or so, I made the leap and tried it out. Here is the kicker: Traditional uniforms come with the badge holder pre-sewn into the shirt. It makes affixing your badge to your uniform easy. This was a no-go for me with the new uniform. Instead of the traditional metal badge that is soldered, hammer-stamped, pumiced, brushed, and polished so that it glistens in the sun, there was a cloth badge already attached to the uniform.

A cloth badge?

In my opinion, a cloth badge is no badge at all. Seriously, if it is bought from a uniform store and made of thread, affixed with Velcro or what have you, then ... "No!"

My badge was made from real metal, so to galvanize the public's trust and to wear over my heart like a shield. It was earned from pure *dedication*. Okay. Yes! It came from a box in a warehouse that some clerk plucked off the shelf and delivered to the graduation ceremony, but for me, standing on stage when the Chief of Police handed me *my* badge and gave me his ten-second spiel, it may as well have been made of solid gold. All that I fought for was *right* there in that shiny piece of tin and guess what? I was wearing it every day, around my neck, pinned to my chest or on my belt. I was representing the department. For those who have forgotten the significance or maybe never understood it in the first place, I'm sorry, but **the badge is a big deal,** and it should be honored as such.

Ok. I'm off my soap box ... for now.

EPILOGUE
Until Valhalla

S hortly after I was bunkered off the scene that fateful day we lost David, I walked aimlessly to a grassy area and sat down. I was out of sorts. Moments later I was approached by my newly assigned critical incident supervisor.

"Hey man! Let's down your gear, so you can relax and cool off."

Yes. That sounds good.

I took off my gear, piece by piece. As my supervisor went to close the tailgate of the Tahoe, I snatched my Kevlar helmet from him. He tried to take it back from me, but I held it tightly to my chest and gave a harsh tug while turning away.

"No!"

I was still armed with my .45 caliber, but the helmet suddenly felt like my security blanket. And, yes, I admit, I have no idea why, of all the gear, the helmet was my sense of "security," but it was. I went back to my happy place on the grass *with* my helmet. My head turned slowly ... back and forth, back, and forth. I could probably have stayed there all night. My sidekick supervisor understood alone time was what I needed most. Only the upper brass was allowed to approach me, along with the other five members of this new brotherhood, a brotherhood to which no one wanted to be a part of. Of course, later, when the dust settled, we were *more* than honored to be. I was briefly able to compose myself, as I watched a sea of blue arrive and scramble about the major intersection we now owned. My composure was short-lived, however, as each commander and chief would approach and offer hugs, thanks, and tears.

Damn it! I just finished bawling and now again and then again.

Some of the kindest words I have ever heard and still use during my responses to these critical incidents are, "I'm glad you're okay."

I was not okay, of course, but over time I would be. There is not a day that will ever pass that I won't think of David. The bad guy fired six rounds that day, three at David and three at me. Dave caught two of the three. I caught zero.

Did I mention? Survivor's guilt sucks.

God forgive me for saying this, but when we lose an Officer, let them not suffer. As for the ones left behind, let us be led by the hand of God, and as for David and the bravest of those who have fallen ... until Valhalla. I love you.

Ephesians 6:16: "In addition to all this, take up the shield of faith, with which you can extinguish all the flaming arrows of the evil one."

Retired Police Officer, Christopher Hoyer is a protector, a survivor, and an advocate for mental, physical, and emotional wellness. After 20+ years as a Street Cop, having been faced with the worst horrors imaginable, he has turned his focus to public speaking, helping the law enforcement community prepare for the trauma that comes with the job. He has spoken to thousands, including first responders, mental health professionals and various professional entities, sharing his story in hopes of saving lives. With two grown children, one grandchild and having retired honorably, the ultimate dream move was recently achieved in San Diego where he now works as a full-time instructor for the Marine Corps Police Academy.

The contents of this book are up for debate. Some of the specified tactics work and some don't. What Hoyer presents here is just one way of doing things, not *the* way. He looks forward to hearing from you, so to continue this important conversation with an open mind and an open heart. He can be reached at chrishoyer46@gmail.com.

Natalie June Reilly graduated cum laude with a Bachelor of Arts degree in Communication from Arizona State University. She is a prolific writer, an author, and a social entrepreneur who, along with her late mother, founded the Nothing but Love Notes initiative. Her efforts have been recognized on Good Morning America, CNN, The Kelly  Clarkson Show, and Woman's World Magazine. On top of which, it's because of a Love Note that she landed the opportunity to edit this book. Natalie has authored two children's books—My Stick Family: Helping Children Cope with Divorce and Pax the Polar Bear: Breaking the Ice. She co-authored *Make it Happen* with Bob Duffy and was the editor for Carol Latham's A Chip Off the Silicon Block. In her early years as a writer, she was a community columnist for the Arizona Republic. Natalie is happily living out her days in Southern California. She can be reached at girlwriter68@hotmail.com.

Made in the USA
Las Vegas, NV
11 October 2021